Teacher's Book of Plays and Choral Readings

Printed on recycled paper.

Macmillan/McGraw-Hill School Publishing Company

New York • Chicago • Columbus

CONTENTS ▷▷▷▷▷▷▷▷▷▷▷▷▷

WRITE YOUR OWN

CHORAL READING

CORRELATIONS ▶▶▶▶▶▶

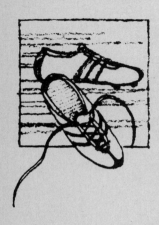

Each play and choral reading selection has been developed to reinforce the unit theme in the Student Anthology

LEVEL 12
UNIT 1/Class Acts

Theme: Developing understanding and insight through experiences related to school

Play: *The Pirates' Funeral*—a dramatic adaptation of several chapters from *The Adventures of Tom Sawyer,* in which Tom and several pals devise an elaborate hoax to teach a schoolmate a lesson.

Choral Reading: *Spelling Bee*—a poem describing the unanticipated outcome of a school spelling bee

UNIT 2/Finders, Seekers

Theme: Personal, historical, and scientific discoveries

Play: *The Treasure Seekers*—a play about a relentless search for sunken treasure that relies on historical research for clues

Choral Reading: *Thumbprint* and *Books Fall Open*—poems that focus on the acquisition of different types of knowledge

UNIT 3/Leave It to Me

Theme: Believing in oneself, self-assurance, and determination

Play: *The Tennessee Tornado*—a dramatization focusing on Wilma Rudolph's incredible determination to overcome paralysis to become the fastest woman in the world

Choral Reading: *It Couldn't Be Done* and *Get a Transfer*—poems that speak to the power of positive thinking

Macmillan/McGraw-Hill

UNIT 4/Timelines

Theme: The influence time has over our lives

Play: *Countdown to Zero*—a fictionalized drama that explores some unexpected consequences resulting from a change in the earth's orbit

Choral Reading: *No Present Like the Time*—a poem that looks at time from a new perspective

UNIT 5/A Place in the Heart

Theme: Individuals finding a place within a family

Play: *The Secret Garden*—a dramatic adaptation of the classic novel in which two unhappy children eventually bloom like the garden they discover

Choral Reading: *Something for Everyone*—a poem that celebrates the diversity of families and lifestyles

UNIT 6/Profiles of Courage

Theme: Turning points that lead to courageous acts

Play: *A Thousand Miles to Freedom*—a play set in 1848 based on the true account of two slaves who devise an ingenious plan to escape from bondage

Choral Reading: Excerpts from *The Call to Arms* and *The Declaration of Independence*—two documents that mark dramatic turning points in our nation's history

v

INTRODUCTION ▶▶▶▶▶▶▶▶

We read for many different reasons, but chief among them should be the discovery that reading can be both fun and purposeful. And what could be more entertaining than working together to make words come alive in a Readers Theater or choral-reading presentation? This book of plays and choral readings has been developed to give you and your students an opportunity to enjoy reading aloud together. At the same time, your students will be developing their reading fluency skills through these enjoyable and motivating oral-reading experiences.

The following pages provide a compilation of hints and tips gathered from teachers who have made oral-reading techniques work in their classrooms. Unlike dramatic productions requiring memorization, elaborate sets, costumes, and stage directions, Readers Theater and choral reading only require a set of scripts and a group of enthusiastic readers—the former you are holding, while the latter wait in the wings of your classroom!

READERS THEATER—A DESCRIPTION

Readers Theater has been used by teachers for many years. Also known as Dramatic Reading, Chamber Theater, or Story Theater, the name Readers Theater seems most appropriate because it puts the emphasis where it belongs—on the *reading* rather than the memorization of a script. Unlike traditional drama in which performers memorize lines and move about a stage, Readers Theater is simply the rehearsed oral reading of a script by a group of performers. It requires no training in drama or the performing arts on the part of students or teachers; there are no complicated guidelines to follow. While simple costumes or backdrops can be used to help establish characterization and setting, they are optional. The fact that Readers Theater involves such simple techniques makes it a viable option for every classroom.

READERS THEATER AND CHORAL READING—THE BENEFITS

Among the chief benefits of Readers Theater and choral reading is the development of oral-reading fluency. Identified by some reading authorities as a frequently "neglected goal" of reading instruction, fluency training has been recognized as an important aspect of proficient reading.

Two essential components for successful fluency training are repeated reading and active listening. Most students can sharpen their active listening skills by attending while the teacher reads aloud for a brief period every day. However, convincing students to repeatedly read the same selection orally until fluency is achieved is quite a different matter. Usually the response is less than enthusiastic.

Enter Readers Theater and choral reading!—both natural partners for fluency training. The oral reading of plays and poetry generates a natural excitement and a willingness to rehearse that enables teachers to integrate repeated reading practice into their instructional program. The goal of a polished performance is a genuinely motivating force that provides a rationale for the fluency training that all students need. Readers Theater and choral reading offer students a *meaningful* context in which to practice expression, shading, phrasing, diction, pitch, and rate, as well as word recognition skills. (For additional information on fluency training and its benefits, see the articles listed in the Bibliography.)

Readers Theater and choral reading also develop active listening skills on the part of both participants and audience. Readers must listen attentively to pick up on cues or to chime in as a member of a group. Audience members also are encouraged to sharpen listening skills as they interpret the dialog and narration to visualize settings and characters that are described rather than visibly presented on stage.

In addition to developing fluency skills, Readers Theater and choral reading can also help students internalize literature, thereby improving their comprehension. Dramatizations enable readers to "become" the characters they play. What better way to reinforce character and plot development than through plays? Dramatizations also expose students to the rich heritage of oral language and storytelling. Through the oral reading of scripts and poetry, students internalize the rhythm of repeated refrains, certain language conventions, and traditional story structure.

A final benefit of Readers Theater and choral reading is derived from the high levels of student interaction and involvement within cooperative learn-experiences, students learn to work together, take turns, listen to each other, and employ group decision-making and problem-solving strategies in casting and production decisions.

Unlike many group activities in which all participants must function on or about the same level to effectively complete the task, a Readers Theater group using the scripts in this book can be composed of students with widely differing reading abilities. The scripts have been written to include roles of varying length and difficulty, enabling students of all ability levels to fully participate and contribute to the achievement of the common goal: a shared oral-reading experience.

LAUNCHING READERS THEATER IN YOUR CLASSROOM

As the following steps indicate, introducing Readers Theater to your class is a straightforward procedure. The only rules are: Keep it simple! and Keep it fun!

1. SCRIPT PREPARATION

Decide when you want to introduce the Readers Theater play within a unit. Then duplicate a copy of the script for each cast member and the director. (Since scripts sometimes have a habit of disappearing, you might make a few extras, just in case.) Students can make construction-paper covers, using the full-page art that precedes each script for decoration, if they wish.

2. ROLE ASSIGNMENT

The plays in this collection were purposefully written with roles requiring varying levels of reading proficiency. Initially you may want to take into account individual reading ability when making role assignments, but once students have become familiar

with a play, roles can and should be switched. Because the characters are read rather than acted, the part of a boy can be read by a girl and vice versa. As students become familiar with Readers Theater, they should be encouraged to assume responsibility for casting decisions as they participate within the cooperative decision-making environment of a Readers Theater group.

3. REHEARSALS

In the first rehearsal, students in the cast should sit together in a Readers Theater group—perhaps gathered around a table—and read through the script to get a sense of the plot and characters. If the play is an adaptation, you may want to read aloud the original story. (Sources for stories that have been adapted appear in the Bibliography.) At this time, roles should be assigned or agreed upon, and students can be encouraged to identify their lines with a transparent highlighter.

Subsequent rehearsals should include paired repeated readings where two characters rehearse their lines together. Having a tape recorder available for these readings will enable students to evaluate their progress. In these early rehearsals, students should focus on word recognition and on listening

for cues. Once these goals have been achieved, attention can be turned to articulation, expression, rate, shading, and phrasing. Invite students to make "reader's notes" in pencil in their scripts. A slash, for example, can be used as a reminder of a pause not indicated by punctuation. An underline can indicate that a word needs special emphasis. These notations can be a valuable aid to oral reading.

During rehearsals, students may decide to add their own personal touches to a script. If the cast decides to add, delete, or alter a speech, this change should be made in all copies of the script.

4. BLOCKING AND FOCUS

In Readers Theater, the performers usually do not move about the stage. However, there are two bits of "stage business" that require rehearsal— where the performers will sit in relation to each other, and where they should look when they are speaking.

Each play is accompanied by a blocking diagram that suggests a seating arrangement. Before the performance, students will need to practice entering, assuming their places on stools or chairs, and exiting. If music stands are available, you may wish to have students use them to hold their scripts during a performance. In some cases, a music stand for the narrator has been suggested in the blocking diagram.

Focus should be an important part of the rehearsal process because, with the exception of a simple gesture or two, focus is the only direct action employed during a Readers Theater presentation. Basically, there are two kinds of focus that students can use: on-stage and off-stage focus. In on-stage focus, the characters look at each other when they speak. In off-stage focus, the characters direct their gaze to a spot on the wall behind the audience. In both types of focus, it is important that students be familiar enough with their lines so their eyes and heads are up rather than buried in a script.

5. PROPS AND COSTUMES

While elaborate costumes and props are not necessary for Readers Theater, even the simplest costumes, such as hats, scarves, or animal ears can help students assume their character. Costume suggestions can be found on the resource pages following several of the plays.

Making background murals or very simple props can help students deepen their understanding of a play. Involvement in discussions about what to emphasize in a drawing or in the scenery or about which free-standing props would suggest the setting (a tree) or occasion (a birthday cake) allows a further involvement and commitment on the part of participants. Either the performers or another group of students acting as stage crew can create the props and costumes.

Hand-held props are not suggested for Readers Theater because the hands should be free to hold the script. For a similar reason, masks should be avoided since they may impair the performers' ability to see the script or project the lines.

6. THE STAGE

Readers Theater does not require a proscenium stage with a curtain, just an open area with enough space for the cast and an audience. A corner of the classroom will work as well as the school auditorium. For plays that lend themselves to puppet dramatizations, simple directions for both the puppets and the stage are included in the resource pages. In staging a Readers Theater puppet show, it generally works best to have one cast read the script while another cast operates the puppets.

7. SHARING THE PERFORMANCE

Readers Theater presentations are meant to be shared, but the audience can range from one person to a packed auditorium. Before the performance begins, you or a student may wish to briefly introduce the conventions of Readers Theater so that the audience understands its role in interpreting dialog to visualize the characters and the action. Students may enjoy making programs, tickets, and posters for the production, especially if another class or parents are invited to attend. On the day of the performance, have the characters enter, take their places, and read!

8. PERFORMANCE FOLLOW-UP

After the performance, suggest that the cast gather to discuss their reading of the play. To guide their discussion, they may use the Self-Evaluation Form. By assessing their own performances as readers, as listeners, and as group members, students can set personal goals to work toward during their next oral-reading experience.

WRITE YOUR OWN READERS THEATER PLAY

After participating in a Readers Theater performance, some students will be eager to write their own plays. The Write Your Own Readers Theater Play resource pages have been designed to guide students through this process.

The teacher resource page presents an overview of the steps and highlights some of the major differences between narrative and drama. Once students understand those differences, they can work with partners or in small groups to complete the student resource pages.

- *Getting Started* guides students in answering the question, "How do I get an idea for a play?"

- *The Plot* defines plot structure and gives a model of a plot outline. Building on the previous worksheet, students develop their own plot outline based on one of the play ideas previously identified.

- *Creating Character Sketches* discusses methods for developing realistic characters and models how to write character sketches.

- *A Readers Theater Script* illustrates the proper format for a script. Additionally, it focuses attention on key questions involving the role of the narrator and the importance of creating dialog consistent with a character sketch.

- *Ready, Set, Write!* is a writing-process checklist to help students keep track of the steps involved in prewriting, drafting, revising, proofreading, and publishing a Readers Theater play.

THE CHORAL-READING EXPERIENCE

Choral reading, like Readers Theater, is an activity that promotes fluency through cooperative effort. In choral reading, speaking and listening are complementary processes—groups of students practice reading poetry for another group to listen to. During practice sessions, the group will need a director, usually the teacher in the early sessions; as students become more experienced with this technique, they can explore taking on the responsibilities of the director.

TYPES OF CHORAL READING

Choral reading promotes fluency by giving support to readers, by providing an opportunity for repeated reading with special attention to rhythm and meter, and by encouraging active listening. The four major types of choral reading are

- refrain
- antiphonal
- line-by-line
- unison

In a poem with a refrain, the verse can be read by a solo voice, by a group (the most common choice), or in combination. In line-by-line choral reading, each line or group of lines is read by a different group or solo voice. Antiphonal choral readings are somewhat like call and response, with one group answering another. Unison readings—perhaps the most difficult of all—are read by the entire group.

The choral readings for each unit have suggestions for groups and solo voices. Your students should first try reading the poems as arranged. After they are familiar with a particular reading, encourage them to try other arrangements or other poems.

Macmillan/McGraw-Hill

SIZE AND ORGANIZATION OF THE CHORAL-READING GROUP

You and your students may want to experiment with the size of the choral-reading group, which will vary depending upon the number of students who want to participate and the particular piece being performed. Most often, members of a group should stand together. Sometimes, readers with solo parts are also part of a group. In these cases, the soloists should stand in the front row of the group. Resource pages suggest arrangements of speakers for choral reading.

THE RESOURCE PAGES

This book includes both teacher and student resource pages. Resource pages follow the plays and always include a blocking diagram for the play. Other resource pages may include costume suggestions and patterns, a pronunciation guide, prop suggestions, puppets, puppet-show directions, sound effects, and audiotaping instructions for radio plays. Resource pages for the choral readings include blocking diagrams. The final resource page is a self-evaluation form for readers and listeners.

BIBLIOGRAPHY

ARTICLES ON READING FLUENCY

ALLINGTON, R.L. 1983. Fluency: The neglected reading goal. *The Reading Teacher* 36:556-61.

BEAVER, J.M. 1982. Say it! Over and over. *Language Arts* 59:143-48.

DOWHOWER, S.L. 1987. Effects of repeated reading on second-grade transitional readers' fluency and comprehension. *Reading Research Quarterly* 22:389-406.

_____. 1989. Repeated reading: Research into practice. *The Reading Teacher* 42:502-7.

KOSKINEN, P.S., and I.H. BLUM. 1986. Paired repeated reading: A classroom strategy for developing fluent reading. *The Reading Teacher* 40:70-75.

MICCINATI, J.L. 1985. Using prosodic cues to teach oral reading fluency. *The Reading Teacher* 39:206-12.

RASINSKI, T. 1989. Fluency for everyone: Incorporating fluency instruction in the classroom. *The Reading Teacher* 42:690-93.

_____, and J.B. Zutell. 1990. Making a place for fluency instruction in the regular reading curriculum. *Reading Research and Instruction* 29:85-91.

SAMUELS, S.J. 1988. Decoding and automaticity: Helping poor readers become automatic at word recognition. *The Reading Teacher* 41:756-60.

The Nightingale, by Hans Christian Andersen. Translated by Eve Le Gallienne. New York: HarperCollins Children's Books, 1985.

ARTICLES ON READERS THEATER AND DRAMATIC READING

ANDERSEN, D.R. 1987. Around the world in eighty days. *Instructor* 97(October): 62-63.

_____. 1989. The shy exclamation point. *Instructor* 98(February): 54.

_____. 1988. The sound of great voices. *Instructor* 97(January): 46-47.

BENNETT, S., and K. BEATTY. 1988. Grades 1 and 2 love readers theater. *The Reading Teacher* 41:485.

BIDWELL, S.M. 1990. Using drama to increase motivation, comprehension and fluency. *Journal of Reading* 34:38-41.

BURNS, G., and E. KIZER. 1987. Audio-visual effects in readers' theater: A case study. *International Journal of Instructional Media.* 14(3): 223-37.

DICKINSON, E. 1987. Readers Theater: A creative method to increase reading fluency and comprehension skills. *The New England Reading Association Journal* 23(22): 7-11.

DOWHOWER, S.L. 1989. Repeated reading: Research into practice. *The Reading Teacher* 42:502-7.

EPPERHEIMER, D. 1991. Readers' Theater and technology: A perfect mix. *The California Reader* 24(Spring): 14-15.

FREEDMAN, M. 1990. Readers Theater: An exciting way to motivate reluctant readers. *The New England Reading Association Journal* 26(Autumn): 9-12.

HOWARD, W.L., and others. 1989. Using choral responding to increase active student response. *Teaching Exceptional Children.* 21(Spring): 72-75.

NAVASCUES, M. 1988. Oral and dramatic interpretation of literature in the Spanish class. *Hispania* 71(March): 186-89.

STEWIG, J.W. 1990. Children's books for readers' theater. *Perspectives* Spring:vii-x.

BOOKS ON READERS THEATER

BAUER, CAROLINE FELLER. *Celebrations: Read-Aloud Holiday and Theme Book Programs.* New York: H.W. Wilson, 1985.

_____. *Presenting Reader's Theater: Plays and Poems to Read Aloud.* New York: H.W. Wilson, 1987.

COGER, LESLIE IRENE, and MELVIN R. WHITE. *Readers Theater Handbook: A Dramatic Approach to Literature.* 3d ed. Glenview, Ill.: Scott, Foresman, 1982.

FORKERT, OTTO MAURICE. *Children's Theater that Captures Its Audience.* Chicago: Coach House Press, 1962.

LAUGHLIN, MILDRED KNIGHT, and KATHY HOWARD LATROBE. *Readers Theater for Children.* Englewood, Colo.: Teacher Ideas Press, 1990.

SIERRA, JUDY, and ROBERT KAMINSKI. *Twice Upon a Time: Stories to Tell, Retell, Act Out, and Write About.* New York: H.W. Wilson, 1989.

SLOYER, SHIRLEE. *Readers Theater: Story Dramatization in the Classroom.* Urbana, Ill.: National Council of Teachers of English, 1982.

_____ . "Readers Theater: A Reading Motivator." In *Selected Articles on the Teaching of Reading.* New York: Barnell Loft, 1977.

BOOKS ON CHORAL READING

AGGERTT, OTIS J., and ELBERT R. BOWEN. *Communicative Reading.* New York: Macmillan, 1972.

GOTTLIEB, MARVIN R. *Oral Interpretation.* New York: McGraw-Hill, 1980.

JOHNSON, ALBERT and BERTHA JOHNSON. *Oral Reading: Creative and Interpretive.* South Brunswick: A. S. Barnes, 1971.

BOOKS ON COSTUMES, MAKE-UP, AND PROPS

ARNOLD, A. *Arts and Crafts for Children and Young People.* London: Macmillan, 1976.

BARWELL, EVE. *Disguises You Can Make.* New York: Lothrop, Lee & Shepard, 1977.

CHERNOFF, GOLDIE TAUB. *Easy Costumes You Don't Have to Sew.* New York: Four Winds Press, 1975.

HALEY, GAIL E. *Costumes for Plays and Playing.* New York: Metheun, 1982.

Make and Play Paperback Set (includes costumes, face painting, hats, masks, and Tee-shirt painting). New York: Franklin Watts, 1990.

McCASLIN, NELLIE. *Shows on a Shoestring: An Easy Guide to Amateur Productions.* New York: David McKay, 1979.

MORIN, ALICE. *Newspaper Theater: Creative Play Production for Low Budgets and No Budgets.* Belmont, Calif.: Fearon Teacher Aids, 1989.

PARISH, PEGGY. *Costumes to Make.* New York: Macmillan, 1970.

PITCHER, CAROLINE, consultant. *Masks and Puppets.* New York: Franklin Watts, 1984.

PURDY, SUSAN. *Costumes for You to Make.* Philadelphia: J.B. Lippincott, 1971.

SOURCES FOR ADAPTATIONS

The Adventures of Tom Sawyer, by Mark Twain. New York: Signet Classic, 1980.

The Secret Garden, by Frances Hodgson Burnett. New York: Dell, 1987.

THE PIRATES' FUNERAL

By JOE CLARO

based on an incident in THE ADVENTURES OF TOM SAWYER BY *Mark Twain*

Cast

Mark Twain	Aunt Polly
Tom Sawyer	Sid Sawyer
Becky Thatcher	Mrs. Harper
Joe Harper	Reverend Sprague
Huckleberry Finn	

MARK TWAIN: My name is Samuel Clemens, but you probably know me by my pen name, Mark Twain. I've been a Mississippi riverboat pilot, a printer, a journalist, and a travel writer—so, as you can see, I've gotten around quite a bit. But most of the events I'm going to tell you about happened either to me or to friends of mine right in my own hometown of Hannibal, Missouri, where I grew up in the 1840s. It wouldn't surprise me one bit, however, if some of the people you're about to meet act just like people you know. Take Tom Sawyer, for instance. Tom lived with his Aunt Polly in St. Petersburg, Missouri. Now Aunt Polly loved Tom dearly, though bringing him up correctly was sometimes a trial, for Tom was full of fun and mischief. He was quick-witted, too, make no mistake about that. On the day I'm thinking of, Tom was at school putting all his wits to the task at hand. Oh no, it wasn't reading or writing he was working so hard at. He was trying to win the admiration of a certain new girl at school—Becky Thatcher—without seeming to be doing so, of course.

TOM: Say, Jeff, want me to learn you how to walk the fence? Come on now, don't be afeard. I can even walk it blindfolded. You stand right here and I'll show you. Now just you watch!

MARK TWAIN: Jeff was mesmerized. But from Becky, there was not so much as a glance. Why if truth be told, Tom had done everything he could think of to make Becky notice him. He'd tried yelling, laughing, throwing handsprings, standing on his head, jumping over the schoolyard fence at risk of life and limb—in short, he'd done just about all the heroic things he could conceive of. But despite his efforts, Becky seemed to be unconscious of it all. Finally, in desperation, he fell tumbling and sprawling under her nose.

TOM: Say, Becky! Becky Thatcher! Just watch me walk on my hands! See?

BECKY: Humph! Some people around here think they're mighty smart—always showing off. Go away and leave me alone, Tom Sawyer! Your childish behavior is just too tiresome.

MARK TWAIN: Poor Tom. His cheeks burned. His eyes filled with tears. Embarrassed by Becky Thatcher in front of all his classmates, he felt forsaken and friendless. As he wandered out of the schoolyard and down Meadow Lane, he could hear the school bell tinkling faintly in the background—it was too late now. He had been driven out into the cold world and had to submit to what cruel fate had in store for him.

TOM: I haven't a friend in the world. Nobody loves me. I reckon I'll just have to leave this place forever. I'll just pick up and go. Then I'll . . . I'll lead a life of crime, that's what I'll do! There's no other choice for a poor, friendless boy. Someday, they'll all be sorry for the way they treated me.

MARK TWAIN: Just at this moment, Tom met his sworn comrade, Joe Harper. Joe was as damp-eyed as Tom and also seemed to have some sad and dismal purpose in his heart.

JOE: Tom! Why aren't you in school? And what are you crying about?

TOM: I'm crying because I've tried to do right and get along, but they won't let me. I've decided to run away from home and never return. I hope at least that you won't forget me, Joe. By the way, why aren't *you* in school? And what are *you* crying about?

JOE: I was looking for you. I wanted to tell you that I'm leaving this place. I just got a whipping for drinking some cream. And I never even saw the stuff! It's plain as day that my ma is tired of me and wants me to go. I guess she'd be better off if I just disappeared. I just hope she'll be happy without me, and never regret forcing her poor boy to suffer and die out here in the unfeeling world.

TOM: Yes, they'll surely miss us, all right. But leaving is the only thing for us to do. Now I've been thinking, and I've got an idea about what we should do once we're free of this place.

JOE: I reckon you do, Tom. You always have ideas. But this time, I've got an idea of my own.

TOM: You do?

JOE: Yes! I'm going to become a hermit.

TOM: A hermit! That's no job for you!

JOE: All the same, it's what I've decided.

TOM: But what will you do?

JOE: I'll go live in a cave. I'll eat crusts of bread that I find on the road at night. Eventually, I'll die of cold and starvation.

TOM: Tarnation, that's a dumb idea if I ever heard one! Come along with me, Joe. I'm going to be a pirate!

JOE: A pirate?

TOM: Why, we'll go plowing over the seas in our black-hulled racer, the *Spirit of the Storm*, with a skull and crossbones flying from the top mast. We'll steal money and jewels from passing ships! And we'll ransom beautiful women, and eat like kings, and wear black velvet suits with crimson sashes and hats with waving plumes!

JOE: That does sound better than starving to death in a cold cave!

MARK TWAIN: Just then, Huckleberry Finn, known as Huck to his friends, appeared around the bend of Meadow Lane. Now Huck was a motherless boy whose father let him run wild. As a consequence, Huck was idle and lawless and vulgar and bad. This, of course, meant that he was envied by all the respectable boys who were under strict orders from their mothers not to play with him because he was such a "bad influence."

JOE: Look, here comes Huck Finn. Should we tell him our plans, Tom?

TOM: Sure, why not? Hello, Huckleberry!

HUCK: Hello, yourself, and see how you like it.

TOM: Huck, Joe and I have just decided to run away and become pirates.

HUCK: Well, that sounds like a good plan.

TOM: Huck, I have an idea. Why don't you come along with Joe and me? Why, you could be Huck Finn, the Red-Handed, and Joe could be Joe Harper, the Terror of the Seas.

JOE: And who will you be, Tom?

TOM: Why, I'll be Tom Sawyer, the Black Avenger of the Spanish Main!

Macmillan/McGraw-Hill

HUCK: When do we leave?

TOM: Right now! No, wait . . . pirates don't sneak off during the day. We'll meet at midnight, and then we'll take off.

JOE: Take off for where?

TOM: Well, let's see now. We want a place we can get to without too much trouble—just as a starting-off point, you understand.

HUCK: And it has to be a place where nobody can bother us.

TOM: I know! We'll head for Jackson's Island. It's only three miles down river. We can swipe a raft and get there in no time.

JOE: Jackson's Island it is! We'll be the bulliest pirates that ever were!

TOM: We'll meet at the big tree on the riverbank, two miles north of town, at midnight, sharp. Bring your fishing lines and hooks and any provisions you can purloin in a dark and mysterious way.

MARK TWAIN: So Jackson's Island was their goal. All that day, Tom and Joe dropped vague hints to certain select friends that pretty soon the town would hear something, but they wouldn't tell what it was. At midnight, Tom showed up at the meeting place carrying a boiled ham. He let out a low whistle. He was answered by two other whistles coming from the dark.

JOE: Who goes there?

TOM: Tom Sawyer, the Black Avenger of the Spanish Main. Name your names.

HUCK: Huck Finn, the Red-Handed.

JOE: Joe Harper, the Terror of the Seas.

TOM: 'Tis well. Give the countersign.

HUCK/JOE: BLOOD!

TOM: Good. I brought a boiled ham. What have you got, Terror of the Seas?

JOE: A side of bacon and some corn pone.

TOM: And you, Red-Handed?

HUCK: I couldn't get any food. But I did bring a skillet.

TOM: Good. Now, let's get the raft.

MARK TWAIN: The raft was tied up not far from where the boys met. They knew all the raftsmen were in the village for the night. Still, they acted as though they might be discovered at any moment.

JOE: Shhh! Move quietly.

TOM: If the foe awakens, let him have it to the hilt!

HUCK: Right. Dead men tell no tales.

TOM: Joe, you take the forward oar. Huck, you're on the after oar.

MARK TWAIN: The three would-be pirates shoved off quietly, with Tom standing in the middle of the raft giving orders. Soon they were drifting past the village they had agreed to leave forever. All three were silent, but their private thoughts were very similar.

TOM: My last look at St. Petersburg. If only Becky could see me now, facing peril and death on the wild sea with a grim smile on my lips. Then she'd be sorry for ignoring me.

JOE: I'll never come back here again. Won't my mother be broken-hearted to know that she drove her boy to a life of crime.

HUCK: I never knowed what it was like to be part of a real family, but St. Petersburg is as much of a home as I ever expect to have. Not anymore, though. Now I'm an outlaw. Outlaws don't have homes. It's just as well. I never *really* liked living civilized, anyways.

MARK TWAIN: It took the boys nearly two hours to reach the island. They waded ashore with their freight, including an old sail that they spread over some bushes for a tent to shelter their provisions. In the meantime, the empty raft began to drift downstream with the current.

HUCK: Grab holda that raft!

JOE: We'd best tie it to a rock.

TOM: Naw, let it go. We won't be needing the raft. This here's our new home.

MARK TWAIN: They all watched the raft slowly drift out of sight. It was as though they had broken the last link between themselves and civilization. As far as the boys were concerned, they were in heaven. They built a roaring fire and used the skillet to cook some bacon and corn pone. When they finished eating, they stretched out on the grass.

JOE: Ain't this terrific?

TOM: It's *great!* What would the other boys say if they could see us now?

JOE: What would they *say?* Well, they'd just die to be here. Don't you think so, Hucky?

HUCK: I reckon so. Anyways, *I'm* suited. I don't want nothing better'n this. I don't ever get as much to eat as we just had. And here they can't come bullying and picking at a feller.

TOM: It's just the life for me. You don't have to get up mornings, and you don't have to go to school, and wash, and all that blame foolishness. See, Joe, I was right. A pirate doesn't have to do *anything* when he's ashore. But a hermit—*he* has to be praying considerable. And then he doesn't have any fun anyway, all by himself that way.

JOE: Yes, that's so. But I hadn't thought much about it, you know. I'd a good deal rather be a pirate, now that I've tried it.

TOM: Sure you would. People don't care much for hermits these days, like they used to in olden times, but a pirate's always respected. Besides, a hermit's got to sleep on the hardest place he can find and put sackcloth and ashes on his head, and stand out in the rain, and . . .

HUCK: What does he put sackcloth and ashes on his head for?

TOM: I dunno. But they've *got* to do it. That's what hermits always do. You'd have to do that if you was a hermit.

HUCK: Derned if I would.

TOM: Why, Huck, you'd *have* to. How would you get around it?

HUCK: Why, I just wouldn't stand it. I'd run away.

TOM: Run away! Well, you *would* be a nice old slouch of a hermit. You'd be a disgrace.

HUCK: What does *pirates* have to do, anyway?

TOM: Oh, they just have a bully time! They capture ships and burn 'em. They get the treasure off the ships and bury it in some awful place on their island, where there's ghosts and things to watch it. And they round up everybody in the ships and make 'em walk the plank.

JOE: Not the women, Tom. Why, pirates are noble! They don't harm the women.

TOM: That's right, they don't hurt the women. They're too noble for that. And the women are always beautiful, too.

JOE: And they wear the bulliest clothes! All gold and silver and covered with diamonds.

HUCK: Who?

JOE: Why, the pirates, of course.

HUCK: Look at what I have on. I reckon I ain't dressed fitten for a pirate. But I ain't got no other clothes but these.

TOM: Don't worry, Huck. We'll all have the finest clothes you can imagine.

HUCK: When?

TOM: Just as soon as we get started pirating.

MARK TWAIN: Gradually, the talk died down and drowsiness began to overtake them. The Red-Handed soon fell asleep. But the Terror of the Seas and the Black Avenger of the Spanish Main had more difficulty dropping off. Neither of them spoke. But their private thoughts showed that they felt a vague fear that they had done wrong to run away, and each had some doubts about pirating.

Macmillan/McGraw-Hill

JOE: This surely is a swell place, but I can't help wondering if we're doing the wrong thing. I stole that side of bacon from Ma's kitchen. I wonder if she knows I'm the one who took it . . . I wonder what she's doing right now . . . I wonder if pirates ever think of the people they left behind. Oh, well, I guess I'd better stop wondering and try to get to sleep.

TOM: Well, we did it. We're pirates. But I wish I hadn't hooked that boiled ham from Aunt Polly. No, I didn't hook the ham. *Hooking* is what I do when I grab a piece of pie. This was *stealing*. And stealing's wrong. Well, it had to be done. From now on, though, we'll be pirates who don't steal anything.

MARK TWAIN: The next morning, the boys caught four fish with their hooks and lines. They feasted on fish and bacon. After breakfast, they chased one another around the island, then they went for a swim in the river. They played a game of marbles, took another swim, and then gradually wandered apart and stretched out on the sand to rest. All three fell to gazing longingly across the wide Mississippi River to where the village of St. Petersburg lay drowsing in the sun. Tom found himself writing "Becky" in the sand with his toe. Joe was getting more homesick by the minute. Even Huck was in a gloomy mood. Suddenly, they were shaken from their thoughts by a deep, booming sound that floated over the water from some distance away.

JOE: What was that?

TOM: I wonder!

HUCK: 'Taint thunder, becuz thunder . . .

JOE: Hark! Listen—don't talk!

TOM: I'll climb this tree and see if I spot anything.

HUCK: Sounded mighty like a cannon to me.

JOE: A cannon?

TOM: I can see it! You know, the little steam ferryboat? It's about a mile below the village, and her deck is crowded with people. And there's a great many skiffs following the ferry. Oh—there's a puff of smoke—they've just fired a cannon over the water!

HUCK: Why would they be doing that?

TOM: I know now! Somebody's drownded!

HUCK: That's it! Remember, they done that last summer when Bill Turner got drownded. They shoot a cannon over the water, and that makes the body float to the top.

JOE: By jings, I wish I was over there now.

HUCK: Me, too. I'd give heaps to know who it is.

TOM: Help me down from here, boys. I know who's drownded.

JOE AND HUCK: Who?

TOM: Why, it's us, of course!

JOE: Us? You're right! They think we drownded!

HUCK: Ha, ha! They're looking for us!

TOM: They think we're dead!

JOE: Oh, this is too good! They miss us! The whole town is out looking for our dead bodies!

TOM: They must be heartbroken! Imagine how bad they must feel about the way they treated us!

HUCK: Tarnation, everybody's probably talking 'bout us. Oh, them other boys must surely be dying of envy!

MARK TWAIN: The boys felt like heroes. They returned to their pirate camp, slapping one another on the back and exchanging congratulations. They caught some fish, cooked it in the skillet, and never stopped talking about the news. But as darkness fell, the talk quieted and turned to other matters.

JOE: What do you two think about some day, maybe, going back to civilization?

TOM: What? Nothing could ever get me to go back there! We're pirates now!

JOE: Well, I didn't mean right away. I meant some day.

TOM: Absolutely not! We'll never go back.

HUCK: Never? Well, I don't know about that. I might go back when I got all them fancy clothes pirates wear.

TOM: Not me! I ain't never going back there!

MARK TWAIN: But Tom wasn't as committed as he made out to be. When Huck and Joe were sound asleep, he tiptoed away from the camp. He found a piece of white sycamore bark, and using a piece of red chalk that he had in his pocket, he wrote a note on it to his Aunt Polly. This was to let her know that he and his friends were safe. On another piece of bark, he wrote a note to Joe and Huck willing them all his earthly possessions if he wasn't back by breakfast. Then he ran to the beach,

Macmillan/McGraw-Hill

waded out as far as he could, and began swimming. Some time later, he reached the shore, three miles below the village.

TOM: Hark! There's the village clock striking ten. I'll rest a few minutes and then go to Aunt Polly's.

MARK TWAIN: Tom slipped through the deserted village streets and surreptitiously made his way to his aunt's house. He was surprised to see lights burning so late at night. He crept to the house and peeked in the window. There sat Aunt Polly, Tom's brother Sid, Joe Harper's mother, and the Reverend Mr. Sprague. Quiet as a cat, Tom slipped unnoticed into the house. Then he crawled under Aunt Polly's bed and listened.

AUNT POLLY: As I was saying, Tom warn't *bad,* so to say, only mischeevous. He warn't any more responsible than a colt. He never meant any harm, and he was the best-hearted boy that ever was. Ohhh, I miss him so!

SID: Don't cry, Aunt Polly.

MRS. HARPER: It was the same with my Joe. Always full of the dickens and up to every kind of mischief, but he was just as unselfish and kind as he could be. And to think I went and whipped him for taking that cream, never once recollecting that I throwed it out myself because it was sour. And I'll never see him again in this world—never, never, never! The poor abused boy!

SID: Well, I hope Tom's better off where he is. But if he'd been better in some ways . . .

AUNT POLLY: Sid! Not a word against my Tom, now that he's gone! God'll take care of him—don't you worry about that! Oh, Mrs. Harper, I don't know how to give him up! He was such a comfort to me, although he tormented my old heart right out of me, almost.

REV. SPRAGUE: The Lord giveth, and the Lord hath taken away.

MRS. HARPER: Blessed be the name of the Lord! But it's *so* hard! Only last Saturday, my Joe busted a firecracker right under my nose, and I knocked him sprawling. Little did I know then how soon . . . Oh, if it was to do over again, I'd hug him and bless him for it.

AUNT POLLY: Yes, yes, yes, I know just how you feel, Mrs. Harper. I know just *exactly* how you feel. No longer ago than yesterday noon, my Tom took and filled the cat full of patented painkiller medicine. I did think the creature would tear the house down. And, God forgive me, I cracked Tom's head with my thimble. Poor boy, poor, dead boy. But he's out of all his troubles now. And the last words I ever heard him say was to reproach me for being so strict with him.

MARK TWAIN: This memory was too much for Aunt Polly. She burst into tears, and Mrs. Harper did the same. Under the bed, Tom was having trouble holding back his own tears. He had to restrain himself from rushing out and overwhelming his Aunt Polly with hugs and kisses.

REV. SPRAGUE: Do not be ashamed of your tears, ladies. It's entirely appropriate to shed tears for the dear departed.

MRS. HARPER: Reverend Sprague, tell us again about the search party.

REV. SPRAGUE: Well, ladies, as you know, at first we thought the boys had merely run off. After all, they had told some of their friends that something surprising would happen soon.

SID: That's Tom, all right. Always a showoff!

REV. SPRAGUE: When we realized the raft was missing, we figured the boys had taken it, and we expected them to turn up just down the river a bit. Then, when we found the raft lodged against the shore some five or six miles downriver from the village, and the boys didn't come home for supper, hope for their safety began to diminish.

SID: Is everybody sure they've drowned?

REV. SPRAGUE: The men are going to continue searching until early Sunday. If the boys haven't been found by then, we'll have to give up, and I'll preach their funerals that morning.

MARK TWAIN: Tom shuddered to hear of plans for his own funeral. He remained motionless under the bed until everyone was gone and Aunt Polly was asleep. He waited until he heard her gentle snoring. Then he stole out from under the bed and stood looking down at his aunt in the dark. His heart was full of pity for her. He took the piece of sycamore bark out of his pocket and placed it by the candle. Suddenly, something occurred to him, and he stood in thought for several seconds. His face lighted with a happy solution, and he put the bark hastily back into his pocket. Then he leaned over, kissed Aunt Polly on the forehead, and made his stealthy exit, latching the door behind him. By dawn, Tom was back at the island. He hid behind a tree and listened as Huck and Joe talked about him.

JOE: No, Tom's true-blue, Huck. He's bound to come back. He won't desert. He knows that would be a disgrace to a pirate, and Tom's too proud for that sort of thing. He's up to something or other. I just wonder what.

HUCK: Well, the things he left behind is ours, ain't they, Joe?

JOE: Pretty near, but not yet, Huck. The note says the things are ours if he ain't back here by breakfast.

MARK TWAIN: With fine dramatic effect, Tom suddenly appeared from behind a tree.

TOM: Which he is!

JOE: Tom! See, Huck? Didn't I tell you he'd be back?

HUCK: Tom, where you been?

TOM: I went back home.

JOE: Back home? And gave away our hiding place?

TOM: Course not! I sneaked in and listened to your mother and my aunt talking about how sad they are now that we're dead.

HUCK: And nobody saw you?

TOM: Nope. I heard the Reverend Sprague tell them how they knew we were dead because they found the raft we swiped. You should have heard the wailing in that room!

JOE: So they've given up looking for us! Hooray!

TOM: Not yet. They'll look until sunrise Sunday morning. Then we'll be officially dead. And you'll never guess what else.

HUCK: What? Tell us! Come on, tell us!

TOM: On Sunday morning, the Reverend Sprague will preach our funerals!

MARK TWAIN: This was better news than Huck and Joe could have imagined. The boys celebrated like heroes. They had a big breakfast and went for a refreshing swim. All the time, they congratulated one another on the success of their plan. Later, they lay stretched out in the woods.

TOM: I bet there's been pirates on this island before, boys. We'll explore the island again. They've hid treasures here somewhere. How'd you like to come upon a rotten chest full of gold and silver?

JOE: Maybe. I don't know. I've been thinking, Tom. Let's give it up. I want to go home. It's so lonesome.

TOM: Oh, no, Joe. You'll feel better by and by. Just think of all the fishing that's here.

JOE: I don't care for fishing. I want to go home.

TOM: But, Joe, there ain't such another swimming place anywhere.

JOE: Swimming's no good. I don't seem to care for it nearly as much as when there's someone like Ma to say I can't go in. I want to go home.

TOM: Oh, shucks! Baby! You want to see your mother, I reckon.

JOE: Yes, I *do* want to see my mother. And you would too, if you had one. I ain't any more baby than you are, so there!

TOM: Well, we'll let the crybaby go home to his mother, won't we, Huck? Poor thing! Does it want to see its mother? And so it shall. *You* like it here, don't you, Huck? We'll stay, won't we?

Macmillan/McGraw-Hill

HUCK: Well, y-e-s. . . .

JOE: I'll never speak to you as long as I live, Tom Sawyer! There now! I'm gonna get dressed.

TOM: Who cares! Nobody wants you to stay anyway. Go 'long home and get laughed at. Oh, you're a nice pirate, Joe Harper! Huck and me ain't crybabies. We'll stay, won't we, Huck? Let him go if he wants to. I reckon we can get along without him, all right.

HUCK: I want to go, too, Tom. It was beginning to get so lonesome. And now, with Joe gone, it'll be even worse. Let's all go.

TOM: I won't! You can both go, if you want to! I mean to stay.

HUCK: Tom, I wisht you'd come, too. Now, you think it over. We'll wait for you when we get to shore.

TOM: Well, you'll wait a blame long time, that's all!

MARK TWAIN: Tom watched Huck and Joe gather their things. And as they began to wade into the river, it suddenly dawned on Tom that Jackson's Island would be a lonely place without his two companions.

TOM: Wait! Wait! I want to tell you something!

JOE: What do you want to tell us, Tom?

TOM: I have a secret plan. I been thinking about it all day. When you hear it, you're not going to want to go anywhere.

HUCK: A secret plan? Well, tell us what it is.

MARK TWAIN: When Tom explained his secret, Huck and Joe cheered and laughed and danced around him.

HUCK: It's a great plan, Tom! I'll stay with you!

JOE: I can't wait! I'm staying, too!

MARK TWAIN: They made their plans, and the mutiny was laid to rest. Then after a hearty supper and some jolly conversation around the fire, the pirates finally fell asleep. Around midnight, the three awoke to a flashing light in the sky. A deep peal of thunder went rolling and tumbling down the heavens, and big raindrops fell pattering on the leaves.

TOM: Quick, boys! Go for the tent!

Macmillan/McGraw-Hill

MARK TWAIN: They stumbled over roots and vines in the dark. One blinding flash after another came, and peal on peal of deafening thunder. A drenching rain poured down, and the rising hurricane drove it in sheets along the ground. One by one, the boys straggled in and took shelter under the makeshift tent they had rigged from the old piece of sail. They were cold, scared, and soaked to the skin. Next morning, they felt rusty and stiff-jointed.

JOE: Tom, this pirating business is beginning to look less and less cheerful every day.

MARK TWAIN: Saturday came and went, and the searchers found no sign of the missing boys. By Sunday morning, all of St. Petersburg was preparing for the solemn funeral. After Sunday school was over, Becky Thatcher stood outside the church talking to Tom's younger brother, Sid.

BECKY: Oh, if only I hadn't been so cruel to him. I wish I had something to remember him by.

SID: Come by the house after the funeral. You can take everything he ever owned—that should be enough to remember him by.

BECKY: Oh, Sid, I know you don't mean that! Just look around. Why, the whole village has turned out for the funeral.

SID: Yes, and they're all talking about what wonderful fellows the three of them were. Everybody's arguing about who saw the three of them last in life and saying that Tom did thus and so, or Joe said this or that!

BECKY: Why, you know that everyone's just looking for some way to remember the boys.

SID: Well, the last time I saw Tom, he was being cuffed by Aunt Polly for something or other. I guess I'll just have to remember him that way forever.

BECKY: Sid Sawyer! You'd better mind your tongue when you're talking about your dead brother.

MARK TWAIN: Inside the church, the Reverend Mr. Sprague waited until everyone was seated. Then he solemnly began the funeral service.

REV. SPRAGUE: We are gathered on this solemn occasion in memory of three of our brethren, who were cut down in the prime of their lives.

AUNT POLLY: Oh, it's so sad!

SID: There, there, Aunt Polly. Don't cry so.

REV. SPRAGUE: We are here to pay our last respects to Thomas Sawyer, Joseph Harper, and Huckleberry Finn.

MRS. HARPER: My boy! My poor, dead boy!

BECKY: Here, Mrs. Harper, take my handkerchief.

REV. SPRAGUE: These three lost lads were among the finest our community has ever known. St. Petersburg will be a poorer place without their sweet and noble presence.

MARK TWAIN: The minister's booming voice drowned out the sobs rising up from the entire congregation. Those members seated in the back of the church, however, were distracted by the creaking sound of the church door as it slowly opened.

REV. SPRAGUE: Let us remember them for all the fine things they did in life. Let us endeavor to be as good as each of these boys was.

MARK TWAIN: The rustling in the back of the church was turning into a small commotion.

REV. SPRAGUE: If only there were some way we could bring these boys back to life . . .

MARK TWAIN: The Reverend Mr. Sprague suddenly stopped speaking. His eyes were riveted on the doorway at the back of the church. Then all heads turned in that direction. Two people fainted. Many more gasped. Finally, the whole congregation rose and stared as Tom, Joe, and Huck came marching up the center aisle.

AUNT POLLY: Tom! It's my Tom! He's come back!

MARK TWAIN: There were shouts about miracles and more noise than anyone had ever heard in church before. The boys strutted proudly to the front of the congregation.

MRS. HARPER: Oh, Joe! Joe, let me hold you!

MARK TWAIN: Aunt Polly smothered Tom in her arms. Mrs. Harper did the same to Joe. Finally, Tom pulled himself free.

TOM: Aunt Polly, it ain't fair. Somebody's got to be glad to see Huck.

AUNT POLLY: And so they shall! *I'm* glad to see him. Come here, Huck, and let me hug you!

MARK TWAIN: Well, Tom's secret plan to return home with his brother pirates and attend their own funerals was a rip-roaring success. But, as you can imagine, it didn't take long before someone asked where the boys had been all this time. Tom was only half through his explanation when Aunt Polly cuffed him on the ear for what he had done. Joe got a similar slap from his mother. Then both boys found themselves being hugged again. Then cuffed again. Then hugged, and cuffed, and hugged. Meanwhile, Huck slipped out of the church.

TOM: Hey, Huck, where you going?

HUCK: I don't care to be cuffed, but even less do I care to be hugged again!

MARK TWAIN: Finally, the whole congregation trooped out of the church and everyone went home.

AUNT POLLY: Tom, dear boy, I've a notion to skin you alive! I was that worried.

TOM: Auntie, I wish I hadn't done it—but I didn't think.

AUNT POLLY: Oh, child, you never think of anything but your own selfishness. You could come all the way over here from Jackson's Island in the night to laugh at our troubles, but you couldn't ever think to pity us and save us from sorrow.

TOM: Auntie, I know now it was mean, but I didn't mean to be mean. I didn't, honest. And besides, I didn't come over here to laugh at you that night.

AUNT POLLY: What did you come for, then?

TOM: It was to tell you not to be uneasy about us because we hadn't got drownded.

AUNT POLLY: I'd give the whole world to believe that, Tom. But it ain't reasonable because you didn't tell me, child.

TOM: Why, you see, when you got to talking about the funeral, I just got all full of the idea of our coming and surprising everyone, and I couldn't somehow bear to spoil it. So I just put the bark I had written on back in my pocket and kept mum.

AUNT POLLY: Bless your heart, child. Give me a kiss and then be off with you.

MARK TWAIN: Undoubtedly, there are those among you who think that Tom received his comeuppance, if not from Aunt Polly, then from his schoolmates. Yes, some might imagine that they would be indignant at the trick the boys had played. Or, perhaps, jealous of the adventure itself and the attention that was subsequently lavished on the boys. But the fact is that Tom had become a hero! Smaller boys than himself flocked at his heels. Boys of his own size pretended not to know he had been away at all, but they would have given anything to have his glittering notoriety. Tom basked in the admiration. It was food and drink to him. He decided that he could be independent of Becky Thatcher now. Glory was sufficient. Yes, indeed, he would live for glory!

BLOCKING DIAGRAM

Arrange eight chairs, as shown. The narrator, Mark Twain, can use a music stand to hold the script.

1. **MARK TWAIN**
2. **SID SAWYER**
3. **BECKY THATCHER**
4. **HUCKLEBERRY FINN**
5. **TOM SAWYER**
6. **JOE HARPER**
7. **AUNT POLLY**
8. **MRS. HARPER**
9. **REVEREND SPRAGUE**

COSTUME SUGGESTIONS

Mark Twain This performer can wear a white shirt, light-colored pants, and a ribbon tie.

Tom Sawyer and Joe Harper The boys can be dressed in overalls or cut-off jeans with suspenders. A straw hat would be a nice addition for Tom.

Huckleberry Finn Huck can wear frayed pants, a somewhat ragged shirt, and a bandana.

Becky Thatcher A frilly blouse and a full skirt with a sash would make an appropriate costume for Becky. She can also wear a large hair ribbon.

Aunt Polly This reader can be dressed in a long skirt and a blouse, with a shawl or apron added.

Mrs. Harper Joe's mother can wear a costume similar to Aunt Polly's with the addition of a hat or bonnet.

Sid Sawyer Sid should be neatly dressed in knickers, a long-sleeved shirt, and a string tie. For knickers, tuck a pair of pants into knee socks and "blouse" each leg at the knee.

Reverend Sprague This performer can wear a white shirt, a dark jacket, and a black ribbon tie.

MAKING A MURAL

A panoramic scene that includes St. Petersburg, the Mississippi River, and a view of Jackson's Island would make an effective backdrop for the Readers Theater performers.

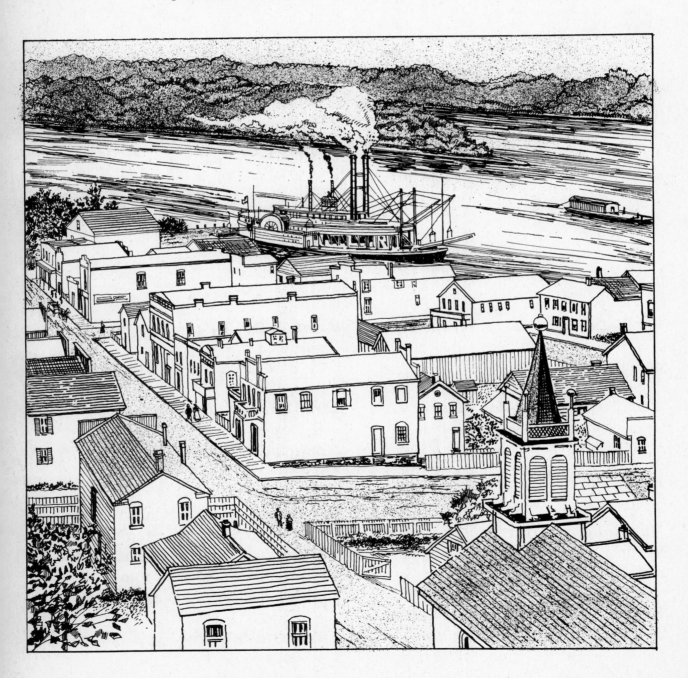

Macmillan/McGraw-Hill

The Treasure Seekers

By Robert Sim

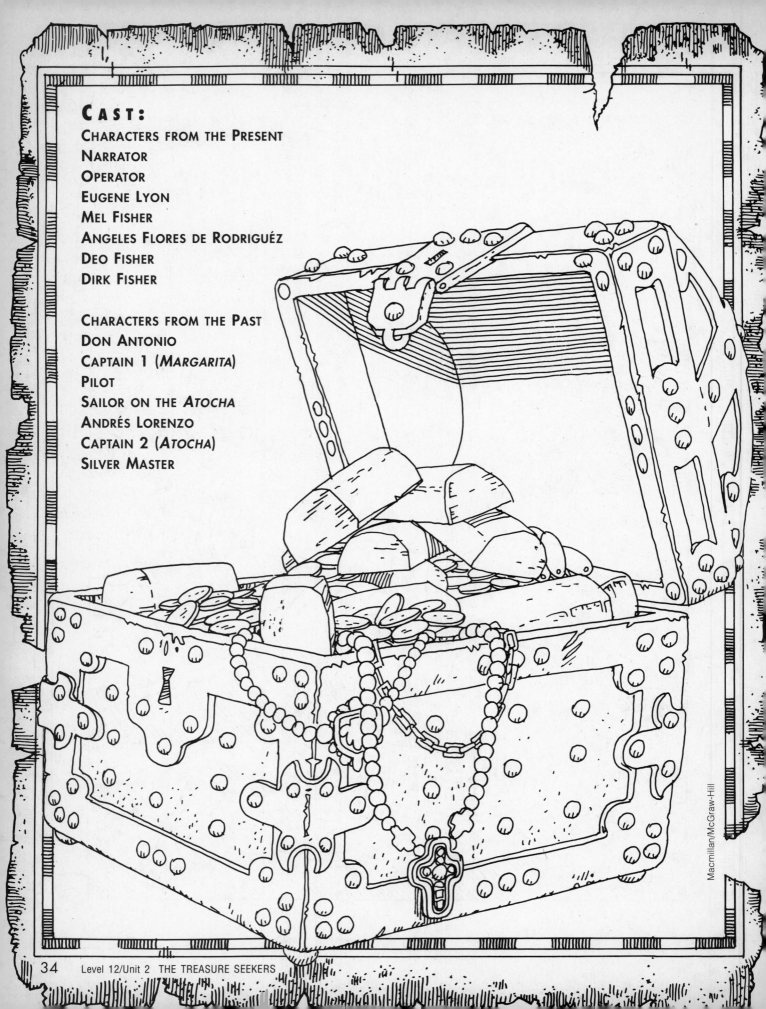

CAST:

CHARACTERS FROM THE PRESENT
NARRATOR
OPERATOR
EUGENE LYON
MEL FISHER
ANGELES FLORES DE RODRIGUÉZ
DEO FISHER
DIRK FISHER

CHARACTERS FROM THE PAST
DON ANTONIO
CAPTAIN 1 (*MARGARITA*)
PILOT
SAILOR ON THE *ATOCHA*
ANDRÉS LORENZO
CAPTAIN 2 (*ATOCHA*)
SILVER MASTER

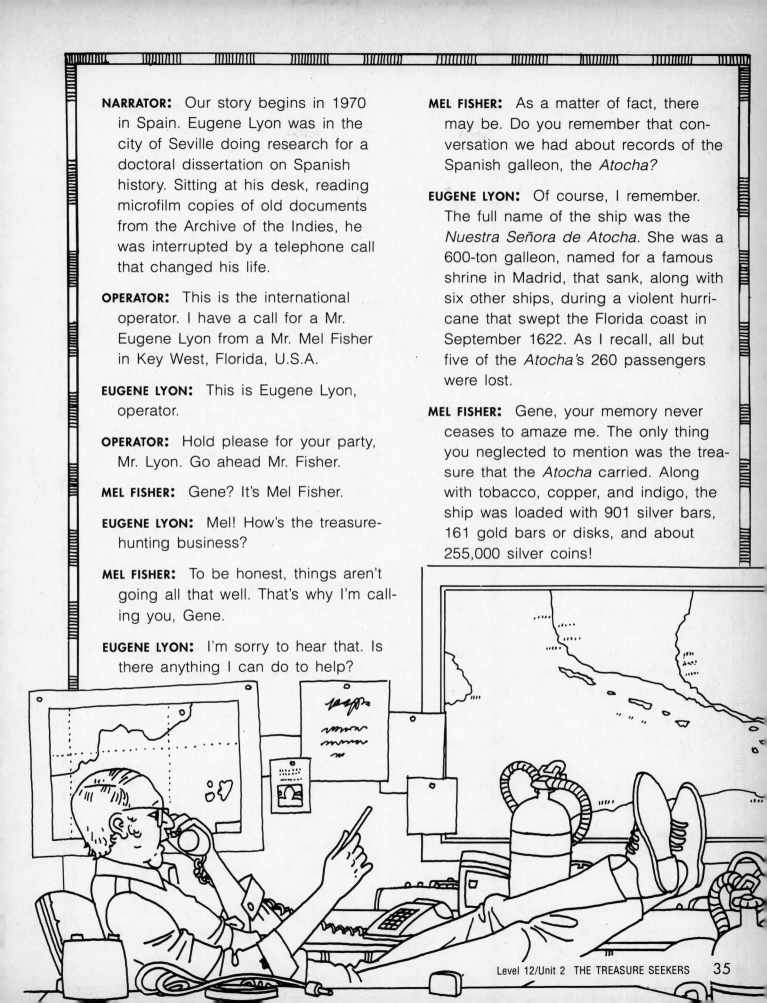

NARRATOR: Our story begins in 1970 in Spain. Eugene Lyon was in the city of Seville doing research for a doctoral dissertation on Spanish history. Sitting at his desk, reading microfilm copies of old documents from the Archive of the Indies, he was interrupted by a telephone call that changed his life.

OPERATOR: This is the international operator. I have a call for a Mr. Eugene Lyon from a Mr. Mel Fisher in Key West, Florida, U.S.A.

EUGENE LYON: This is Eugene Lyon, operator.

OPERATOR: Hold please for your party, Mr. Lyon. Go ahead Mr. Fisher.

MEL FISHER: Gene? It's Mel Fisher.

EUGENE LYON: Mel! How's the treasure-hunting business?

MEL FISHER: To be honest, things aren't going all that well. That's why I'm calling you, Gene.

EUGENE LYON: I'm sorry to hear that. Is there anything I can do to help?

MEL FISHER: As a matter of fact, there may be. Do you remember that conversation we had about records of the Spanish galleon, the *Atocha?*

EUGENE LYON: Of course, I remember. The full name of the ship was the *Nuestra Señora de Atocha.* She was a 600-ton galleon, named for a famous shrine in Madrid, that sank, along with six other ships, during a violent hurricane that swept the Florida coast in September 1622. As I recall, all but five of the *Atocha's* 260 passengers were lost.

MEL FISHER: Gene, your memory never ceases to amaze me. The only thing you neglected to mention was the treasure that the *Atocha* carried. Along with tobacco, copper, and indigo, the ship was loaded with 901 silver bars, 161 gold bars or disks, and about 255,000 silver coins!

EUGENE LYON: I have a suspicion that's what *you're* interested in. Right?

MEL FISHER: Exactly right. I'm calling to ask you to spend some more time looking through the old records and ship manifests at the Archive of the Indies there in Seville. Somewhere there has to be a clue to the whereabouts of that galleon.

EUGENE LYON: I don't know, Mel. You have to understand that the records from the period are incomplete at best. And as I remember, to make things even worse, many of the documents are riddled with wormholes!

MEL FISHER: Gene, those old manifests and documents contain everything we know about the *Atocha*. There must be something in there—some small, unnoticed detail that will give us a clue as to where the ship went down.

EUGENE LYON: Well, I just don't want you to get your hopes up, Mel. The best information we have about the fleet location is secondhand, and it was written four years after the ships sank.

MEL FISHER: You mean the reports by that Cuban agent of the crown? What was his name . . . Melián?

EUGENE LYON: Exactly. Remember, Melián was in the salvage business

himself. He had a lot to lose by accurately reporting the location of the ships that went down in that hurricane.

MEL FISHER: Okay, that's a good point. I guess if I were in his place, maybe I'd be a little vague about the whereabouts of those sunken galleons loaded with gold and jewels!

EUGENE LYON: Did you say, maybe?

MEL FISHER: All right, you've got me there! Sure, I'd keep the information to myself! But Melián's reports to the Spanish court did say without question that the *Atocha* and her sister ship the *Santa Margarita* went down six to ten miles west of Florida.

EUGENE LYON: Correct. They supposedly sank near the atoll called *Cayos del Marquéz,* which today is called the Marquesas Keys.

MEL FISHER: Unfortunately, the ocean in that area is dotted with hundreds of little islands and reefs. I've spent years combing the Atlantic looking for the *Atocha* and the *Santa Margarita,* and I'm no closer today than when I started. Will you look at those records once more?

EUGENE LYON: All right, Mel. Lucky for you, I'm working with an excellent researcher—Angeles Flores de Rodriguéz. Her knowledge of the archives here in Seville and her ability to read and translate these old documents should help speed things up. She and I will review the documents once more, but I just want you to be

prepared: I really don't expect to find anything more that will help you.

MEL FISHER: Gene, I'm convinced that the answer to this mystery is in those records somewhere. I just know it, and if we actually find the *Atocha* and the *Margarita,* it could be worth millions, maybe tens of millions.

EUGENE LYON: Okay, Mel. I'll look. But remember, from my point of view, there's much more than gold and silver at the end of this search. Finding those two shipwrecks would be like passing through a doorway into one of Spain's great moments in history.

MEL FISHER: Remind me of that line next time my partners ask me about the return on their investment.

EUGENE LYON: Okay, Mel. I'll look. I'll look.

NARRATOR: A week later, Eugene Lyon found himself in the Archive of the Indies blowing the dust off three-hundred-year-old documents. It was all at his fingertips: passenger lists, a detailed account of the cargo, even a schedule of where the fleet stopped and where it was headed. After all, the reign of King Philip IV was among the wealthiest in the history of Spain. Great fleets of mercantile ships sailed from Europe to South America, North America, and as far away as the Philippines. Careful records had to be kept.

SEÑORA FLORES: Buenos días, Señor Lyon.

EUGENE LYON: Buenos días, Señora. Are you ready to take another look at the documents dealing with the *Atocha* and the *Santa Margarita?*

SEÑORA FLORES: Your friend Mel Fisher certainly is persistent.

EUGENE LYON: That's why he's one of the best salvage operators in the business. He never gives up. Why don't we start with the eyewitness accounts of the sinking of the *Atocha?*

SEÑORA FLORES: Here you are.

EUGENE LYON: A little I can live with. Now let's see: This account is from 1626; this one is from 1624. . . . Ah, here we are: 1622, the story of Don Antonio de Velasco, one of the survivors.

EUGENE LYON: [*coughing*] I knew when I became a historian that I would search for meaning in the dust of history, but I never expected this much dust!

SEÑORA FLORES: These books are older than your country, Señor. You have to expect a little mold and mildew after three hundred and fifty years!

SEÑORA FLORES: As a soldier aboard the *Santa Margarita,* he knew much about the ship's cargo and destination; but when it comes to the actual shipwreck, he's not very helpful.

EUGENE LYON: Well, I'm not surprised when you consider that he was fighting for his life as the ship tore apart during a hurricane. But what he does tell us provides some clues. Let's look at his story again.

DON ANTONIO: My name is Don Antonio de Velasco. I serve His Majesty Philip, king of Spain, aboard the imperial galleon *Santa Margarita*. I am of noble birth, but I serve my king as a common soldier to gain military experience. I hope to return to the Indies one day, and a soldier's knowledge will serve me well.

CAPTAIN 1: At court there is time for idle chatter, but not on board my ship. If you have nothing to do, speak up. I am sure I can keep you busy.

DON ANTONIO: No, Captain. I am charged with guarding these silver ingots. They are very valuable and . . .

CAPTAIN 1: Then guard them. Don't talk to them. Have you seen the fleet pilot?

DON ANTONIO: Sí, Captain. He approaches now from the captain's walk.

PILOT: Good day, Captain.

CAPTAIN 1: Is it, Señor Pilot? There are great black clouds in the heavens. The seas rise and chop at our decks.

PILOT: It is to be expected, Captain. It is September, and we are well into hurricane season.

CAPTAIN 1: Havana is a comfortable place to wait out the winter, Señor Pilot.

PILOT: Captain, you know the value of your cargo. It would cost the king too much if we waited until spring to sail. King Philip is dependent upon the treasure stored in your holds to pay the war debts owed by the crown. Besides, I told you that if the new moon brought calm seas, our journey would be safe. The new moon was last night, and the waves rolled gently. We have nothing to fear.

CAPTAIN 1: I wish I could share your confidence in the moon. We are over-burdened with cargo and short on crew. Many of our men are sick with fever. Many others have deserted, wishing to spend the winter in these lush surroundings.

PILOT: When the governor finds and hangs them, Havana will look like any other grave. We must set sail, Captain, while our stores are full of food and drink.

CAPTAIN 1: Our stores are full of gold and silver, too. Let me remind you that, with all that extra weight, the *Santa Margarita* will not maneuver well in rough water.

PILOT: With you at the helm, what have we to fear?

CAPTAIN 1: You have the silvery tongue of a courtier, Señor Pilot!

PILOT: Then we sail?

CAPTAIN 1: We sail.

PILOT: Good, I will see that the other captains are informed of this decision.

CAPTAIN 1: Antonio, inform our distinguished passengers that we bid Havana goodbye at high tide.

DON ANTONIO: What of my post, Captain? The silver. . . ?

CAPTAIN 1: I'll watch the ingots while you do as I command.

DON ANTONIO: Sí, Captain.

CAPTAIN 1: Now that Antonio is gone, I can check my own horde of silver. Good. It is all there. We carry so much illegal cargo aboard the *Santa Margarita* and also aboard the *Atocha* that we could use another ship just for the contraband. It's a heavy load, but it will make me a wealthy man.

DON ANTONIO: I have informed the governor, the bishop, and our other passengers of your intention.

CAPTAIN 1: They were pleased?

DON ANTONIO: Yes, but worried about the weather. The bishop is concerned that the hurricane season has begun.

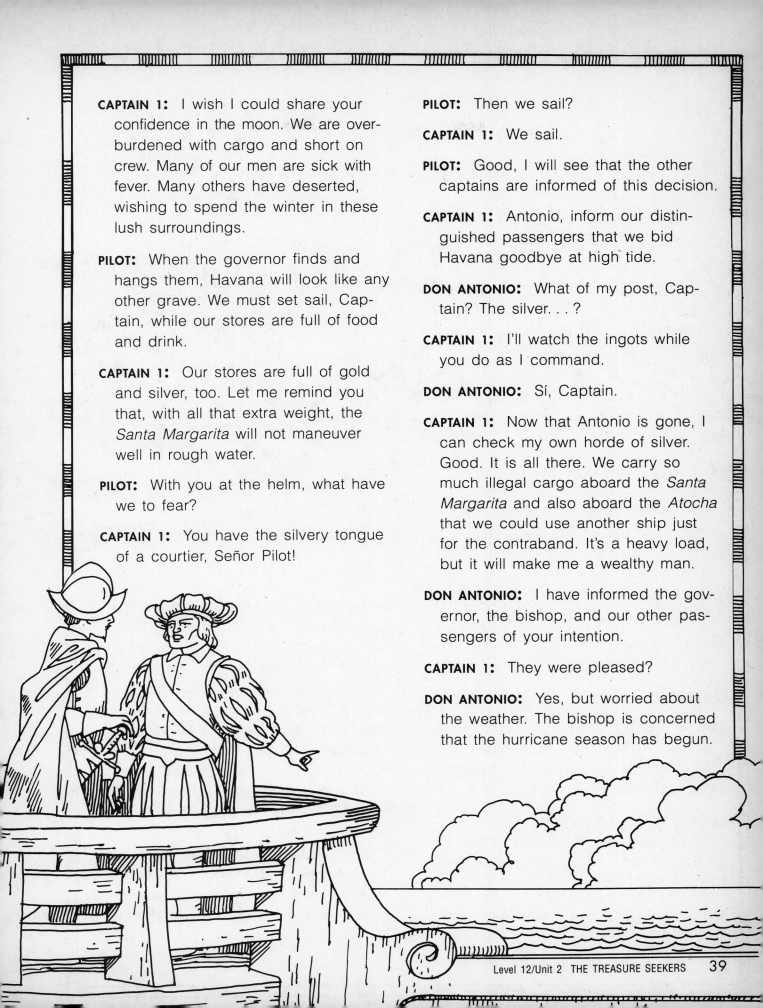

CAPTAIN 1: He is right, but the *Santa Margarita* is a fine oaken ship that has weathered many storms between Spain and the Indies. Our guests— and you for that matter—should worry more about the Dutch Armada. If we run into their warships, it will be life or death, of that you can be sure.

SAILOR: Captain, I bear a message from the *Atocha*.

CAPTAIN 1: Go on.

SAILOR: Our escort of eight armed ships is ready in the bay. The *Atocha* is fully laden with supplies and awaits your command.

CAPTAIN 1: Tell your captain that the *Santa Margarita,* the queen of the sea, will set her sails for Spain at the highest tide.

SAILOR: Sí, Captain. Praise Philip, King of Spain.

DON ANTONIO: The words of the *Atocha* sailor and the words of my own captain rang in my ears as we hoisted anchor and sailed away from Havana. The wind was full in our sails as we joined the great armed argosy beginning its perilous journey. The captain was right. The gold and silver— far more, it seemed, than the load recorded on our manifest—made our ship lie deep in the water. The bales of cotton, the chickens and turtles that would feed us, even the passengers in their gold chains and jewelry weighed less than the piles of gold and silver bars stacked below deck.

NARRATOR: The first-hand account of Don Antonio was not new to Gene Lyon or Señora Flores. Each time they read the story, they came to the same conclusion.

SEÑORA FLORES: There is the information showing that the passengers were nobility. They had jewels with them and lengths of gold chains.

EUGENE LYON: Gold was the currency of the day. If a nobleman or official needed to pay someone . . .

SEÑORA FLORES: . . . or bribe someone . . .

EUGENE LYON: . . . or bribe someone, he just took a link off a gold chain—instant money. But do you know what troubles me? I still cannot understand why they waited until the first week in September to begin their journey back to Spain. September is notorious for hurricanes and tropical storms. Why did they wait so long?

SEÑORA FLORES: Maybe the lack of a crew or the late arrival of an important passenger delayed them. After all, the governor of Venezuela was aboard. If he told them to wait, they would have to obey.

EUGENE LYON: It's another mystery that will never be solved.

SEÑORA FLORES: Maybe we should concentrate on what we do know.

EUGENE LYON: Agreed. Don Antonio's account has them heading north, presumably toward the Gulf Stream.

SEÑORA FLORES: You know, we have another eyewitness report from one of the five survivors of the *Atocha*—a seaman named Andrés Lorenzo.

EUGENE LYON: I've read it so many times I've almost memorized it; but let's have another look. Here it is, in this packet tied with a faded pink ribbon. Let's see . . .

ANDRÉS LORENZO: All was going well aboard the *Atocha*. The seas were rough, but all hands were seaworthy and true. We made good time out of Havana, and the first night passed without incident—and without sleep, at least for me. On the second day, the wind and rain increased steadily. The captain, while outwardly calm, showed signs of inner fear. He asked repeatedly for the men atop the mast to sight and report the whereabouts of the *Santa Margarita*.

CAPTAIN 2: Can you see her?

SAILOR: Sí, Captain, her mast is splintered. The topsail is spread across her deck, covering the wheel and blinding the crew, who are hacking at rope and sail and wood like wild men.

SILVER MASTER: You were wise, Captain, to order our sails lowered.

CAPTAIN 2: Wise in that, yes, but a fool to have left Havana. Silver Master, tend well to your treasure. Our brothers aboard the *Santa Margarita* will not survive this night.

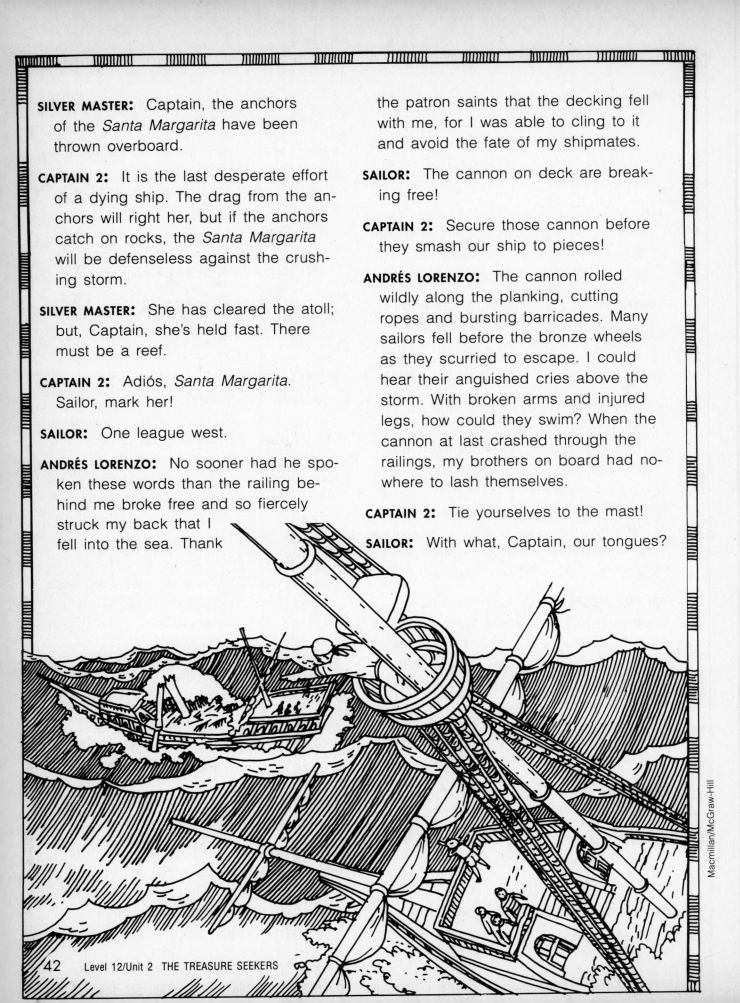

SILVER MASTER: Captain, the anchors of the *Santa Margarita* have been thrown overboard.

CAPTAIN 2: It is the last desperate effort of a dying ship. The drag from the anchors will right her, but if the anchors catch on rocks, the *Santa Margarita* will be defenseless against the crushing storm.

SILVER MASTER: She has cleared the atoll; but, Captain, she's held fast. There must be a reef.

CAPTAIN 2: Adiós, *Santa Margarita.* Sailor, mark her!

SAILOR: One league west.

ANDRÉS LORENZO: No sooner had he spoken these words than the railing behind me broke free and so fiercely struck my back that I fell into the sea. Thank the patron saints that the decking fell with me, for I was able to cling to it and avoid the fate of my shipmates.

SAILOR: The cannon on deck are breaking free!

CAPTAIN 2: Secure those cannon before they smash our ship to pieces!

ANDRÉS LORENZO: The cannon rolled wildly along the planking, cutting ropes and bursting barricades. Many sailors fell before the bronze wheels as they scurried to escape. I could hear their anguished cries above the storm. With broken arms and injured legs, how could they swim? When the cannon at last crashed through the railings, my brothers on board had nowhere to lash themselves.

CAPTAIN 2: Tie yourselves to the mast!

SAILOR: With what, Captain, our tongues?

CAPTAIN 2: Your insolence condemns you!

SAILOR: Captain, you command dead men. Make your peace. We must all say our prayers.

ANDRÉS LORENZO: I watched the pounding storm take my shipmates to their graves. Listing badly to port, her oaken beams screaming in the wind, the *Atocha* made a small circle as though smoothing a place to sleep. All that gold and silver held her low in the water. And when the sea reached up finally, it was like a monster, and with a monster's fatal hand, it pulled her down.

NARRATOR: The deep silence in the library where Señora Flores sat with Gene Lyon went undisturbed for several moments. Only a clock striking the hour broke the quiet.

SEÑORA FLORES: May they rest in peace.

EUGENE LYON: Not if Mel Fisher has anything to say about it, Señora!

SEÑORA FLORES: You have trouble with this expedition, Señor Lyon?

EUGENE LYON: Let's just say that, as a historian, there are times when I am in conflict with some of the goals and methods of treasure hunters. There are some real differences of opinion about shipwreck salvage, you know.

SEÑORA FLORES: So, why do you help him?

EUGENE LYON: Sometimes, I wonder; but I really think that I want to locate the *Atocha* and the *Margarita* as much as Mel. If he does find them, these ships would present us with a unique time-capsule view into Spanish colonial trade and shipboard life.

SEÑORA FLORES: I wish you much success, Señor. Perhaps Lorenzo's account of where the shipwreck occurred will help you.

EUGENE LYON: Yes, with the most famous incomplete sentence in the history of treasure hunting.

SEÑORA FLORES: "One league west"... but where was the *Atocha?*

EUGENE LYON: If we knew, we'd have the answer to our mystery. At least we know that the *Margarita* and the *Atocha* went down within sight of each other.

SEÑORA FLORES: The *Margarita* went down just east of the Cayos del Marquéz, the Marquesas Keys.

EUGENE LYON: Yes, and the *Atocha* went down somewhere nearby. So why, after fifteen years, has Mel Fisher discovered nothing in this area but a few silver coins and a lot of seashells?

SEÑORA FLORES: What did Lorenzo do when he finally got back to Spain?

EUGENE LYON: Well, he probably didn't sign on for any more trips to the Indies! But seriously, why do you ask?

SEÑORA FLORES: Perhaps he wrote other letters about the *Atocha* to relatives or friends.

EUGENE LYON: I doubt it, Señora Flores. After all, Lorenzo was just a seaman. I think our best bet would be to look at the account of Captain de Lugo, commander of the infantry force on the *Santa Margarita*. He survived, and his eyewitness report of the *Atocha*'s sinking says it took place "east of the last key."

SEÑORA FLORES: I know that report well, Señor. Remember, I sent Mr. Fisher a transcript of the document some time ago.

EUGENE LYON: I remember. But I'm wondering if there is something else in the document that might have been missed. Why don't we look at it together one more time?

NARRATOR: After a considerable wait, a *portero* at the Archive of the Indies handed the two researchers a fragile bundle of documents.

EUGENE LYON: Well, here we go. This old-fashioned *procesal* script written without punctuation sure makes these documents hard to read. . . . Wait, here we are. . . . Hold everything! Take a look at this!

SEÑORA FLORES: Yes, that is the section.

EUGENE LYON: But look at what it says— "*veste del último cayo.*" It says *veste*,

not *este*! *West* of the last key, not east! The word must have been copied incorrectly during the transcription process. This means that Mel has been looking on the wrong side of the Marquesas! I'd better let him know right away!

NARRATOR: Meanwhile, back in Florida, Mel Fisher, his wife, Deo, and his son Dirk, were planning the search operation for the upcoming week.

DEO FISHER: Mel, didn't you say that Gene Lyon had hoped to send a report this week?

MEL FISHER: He was supposed to. I've been waiting to see what he'd come up with before doing any planning for this week's exploration. But I don't think we can wait any longer. What do you think, Dirk?

DIRK FISHER: If it were up to me, Dad, I would continue to work in the same area—east of the Marquesas Keys.

DEO FISHER: We're practically past the last reef in that location. In another week, there won't be anywhere else to look.

MEL FISHER: Don't I know it, Deo. Eleven years of exploration and no results! Gene Lyon is our last hope.

DEO FISHER: Gene, if you could hear me, I'd say, "Keep at it!"

NARRATOR: It was just then that the phone rang.

OPERATOR: This is the international operator. I have a collect call from a Mr. Eugene Lyon in Seville, Spain. Will you accept the charges?

MEL FISHER: Yes, operator, I'll accept them. Hello, Gene! I've been wondering what you were up to.

EUGENE LYON: Sit down, Mel. I've got some bad news . . . and some good news. The bad news is that you've been looking on the wrong side of the Marquesas for the last four months.

MEL FISHER: Great. So, what's the good news?

EUGENE LYON: The good news is that I think we've finally tracked down the information you've been looking for.

MEL FISHER: So . . . don't keep me in suspense!

EUGENE LYON: You need to look on the *west* side of the last key of the Marquesas. I hope it's what you're looking for, Mel. If it is, will you promise me you'll preserve the sites until marine archaeologists have a chance to examine the wrecks?

MEL FISHER: We've danced this dance before, Gene. You know I want to conduct the recovery operation professionally. But you have to understand that I've got the pressure of investment partners who want a financial return as soon as possible. I've made a lot of commitments to get financing for this operation.

EUGENE LYON: I'm coming to Florida within the next few weeks, Mel. I hope we can take up this issue again when I see you.

MEL FISHER: I hope we have a reason to take up the issue. See you then, Gene. And thanks!

DEO FISHER: What did Gene have to say, Mel?

MEL FISHER: He's got some revised information that suggests a new location for the *Atocha* and the *Santa Margarita!* Here, I wrote it down.

DIRK FISHER: Let me see it. *West?* West of the Marquesas Keys? Nobody's looked there!

MEL FISHER: Nobody until now. Outfit the *Southwind,* pronto, Dirk. We're going hunting! Today's the day!

DIRK FISHER: Aye, aye!

MEL FISHER: Deo, would you get in touch with our salvage lawyer? Tell him we might be putting in a claim.

DEO FISHER: Of course, but do you really think it's wise to move the whole operation based on a thirty-second telephone call? What proof did he give you?

MEL FISHER: Deo, you've got me there. Gene didn't offer any proof, but I'm sure he'll fill us in on all the details. Trust me—Eugene Lyon takes this history business very seriously. He researches, checks his facts, and always bases theory on evidence. If he says look west, we look west.

NARRATOR: Mel immediately shifted his operations to the west of the Marquesas. He searched during the fall and winter months without success. Then on June 1, 1971, a metal-detecting instrument called a magnetometer, used by Mel in his salvage operations, registered a strong contact. Mel and his divers found some silver coins, a musket ball, a galleon anchor, and three lengths of gold chains. More finds were made during the summer, but nothing to indicate the *Atocha* or the *Santa Margarita* had been located. Still another year passed. Getting funding for the operation became more difficult, but Mel never gave up hope. Always an optimist, he gave T-shirts to the crew with his motto: "Today's the day!" and he sincerely believed it. Finally, in the spring of 1973, his luck began to change.

MEL FISHER: You bet our luck began to change! In one week in May, we hit something we dubbed the "Bank of Spain." On one day alone, fifteen hundred pieces of eight were brought up from the bottom! But I was convinced that the best was yet to come. And that Fourth of July, my hunch proved to be correct.

DIRK FISHER: Dad! Hey, Dad! One of the divers has brought up something that looks like a loaf of bread!

MEL FISHER: Loaf of bread? Why, that's no loaf of bread! That's a silver ingot.

DIRK FISHER: Whatever it is, it weighs a ton. Somebody help me get it over the side of the boat.

DEO FISHER: Look! Here come two more.

MEL FISHER: Quick, hand me something to wipe away the silver sulfide crust. Can anybody make out the marks? It looks like initials and Roman numerals.

NARRATOR: Mel immediately called in Gene Lyon.

EUGENE LYON: Oh, what a thing of beauty! Those are the tally numbers and shipping identification marks you're looking at. Mel, I think this may be it—you may have found your treasure at last!

MEL FISHER: Is there any way to be sure, Gene?

EUGENE LYON: Well, theoretically, we should be able to match the tally number, the weight, and the silver fineness of each bar with the figures recorded in the ship manifests. These three bars are numbered 569, 794, and 4,584. If these ingots were carried on the *Atocha* or the *Santa Margarita,* we ought to be able to find confirmation in the microfilm copy of the manifests.

NARRATOR: Gene Lyon spent the next four days hunched over the microfilm reader in the Key West public library. Without success, he scanned the manifest of the *Margarita.*

EUGENE LYON: Mel, I've got some bad news. I've gone through every page of the manifest for the *Santa Margarita*—those three bars aren't listed in the documents.

MEL FISHER: You've still got the records of the *Atocha,* right? I'm not giving up hope yet. Keep at it, Gene, and think positive!

EUGENE LYON: I'll be back at the library when the doors open on Monday morning.

NARRATOR: On Monday, Gene carefully threaded the microfilm into the viewer and slowly began to turn the crank. The documents listing the treasure loaded on the *Atocha* at the port of Havana yielded no results; the bars were not listed in the manifest.

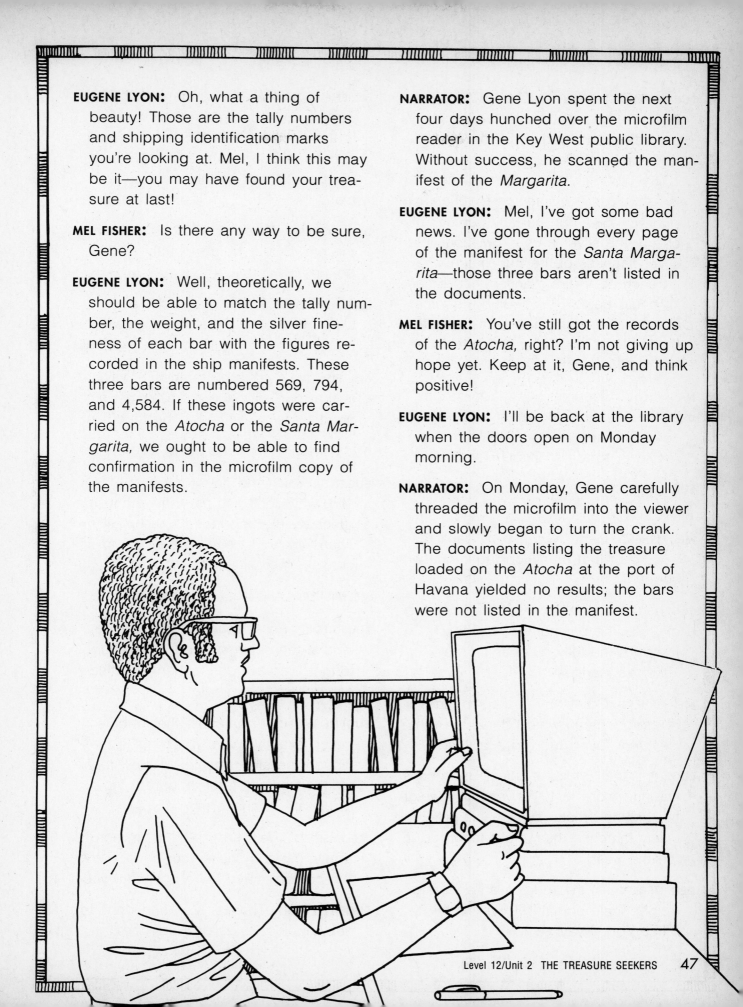

EUGENE LYON: Well, this is it. We're down to the last possibility—the records of the loading of the *Atocha* at the port of Cartagena. After this, I call it quits for the . . . Whoa! There it is—*quatro mill quinientos e ochenta e quatro*: 4,584. It's the tally number of one of the silver bars! Now, does the silver fineness of the bar match what is recorded in the manifest? Let's see, it should be 2,380. . . . Bingo, another match! Fine, pure silver! And now for the last test. I'd better get over to Mel's office right away.

NARRATOR: Gene quickly made a copy of the manifest document page in the library's reader-printer, and then hurried over to Mel's office.

EUGENE LYON: Mel, take a look at this document!

MEL FISHER: Gene, you know I can't read a word of that funny-looking *procesal* script!

EUGENE LYON: Well, look at the spot I've circled. The bar number, 4-5-8-4, matches the tally number on the *Atocha*'s manifest!

MEL FISHER: Great day in the morning! Does this mean what I think it means? Have we found the Big A at last?

EUGENE LYON: I think it does! But there's still one more test. We've got to weigh the bar and make sure that it precisely matches the weight recorded in the manifest.

DEO FISHER: I'll track down an accurate freight scale and get it over to the office right away.

EUGENE LYON: While you do that, I'll work on converting the weight listed in the document as 125 marks and 3 ounces in Spanish measure. Dirk, maybe you can double-check my math.

DIRK FISHER: Based on my calculations, the bar should weigh exactly 63.58 pounds.

EUGENE LYON: That's what I come up with, too. Now we just have to wait until Deo returns with that freight scale.

MEL FISHER: Over sixty pounds of silver in that bar—and there are almost nine hundred more waiting to be found!

DEO FISHER: Here's the scale, Gene.

EUGENE LYON: And now for the acid test. Mel, why don't you set the weight at precisely 63.6 pounds on the scale. Then Dirk and I can lift the bar up onto the weighing platform.

MEL FISHER: All right. Here goes.

NARRATOR: For a second, the balance arm of the scale swayed back and forth . . . it wavered . . . then it settled squarely in the middle.

EUGENE LYON: It matches; the weights match exactly! What a feeling. It's as though the silver master of the *Atocha* reached across three hundred and fifty years to shake my hand.

MEL FISHER: Well, I'd like to reach across a few feet and shake your hand, Gene! We couldn't have done it without you.

EUGENE LYON: Thanks, Mel, and don't forget Angeles Flores de Rodriguéz, my

colleague at the Archive of the Indies in Seville. For that matter, you owe a real debt of gratitude to Captain de Lugo.

MEL FISHER: I'll offer a toast in his honor, right after I call my salvage lawyer!

NARRATOR: For Mel Fisher, his partners, and employees, the next few years were some of the busiest and most stressful of their lives.

MEL FISHER: I'll say it was stressful. The three silver bars were just a beginning. It took us until May 1980 to find the actual site of the shipwrecked *Atocha!*

EUGENE LYON: You mean what we *thought* was the *Atocha*. But when we matched the numbers on the gold and silver bars we uncovered at the site with the 1622 ship documents, we discovered they were listed on the *Santa Margarita* manifest! We had located the *Santa Margarita,* not the *Atocha!*

DEO FISHER: And what a find that was! That wreck yielded over 140 pounds of gold and 1,670 pounds of silver.

MEL FISHER: But the best was yet to come! Five years later, on July 20, 1985, we found the "Mother Lode"— the resting place of the *Atocha's* main treasure mass! There were millions of dollars worth of gold, silver, emeralds, copper, and brass.

EUGENE LYON: The shipwrecks gave archaeologists a wealth of information. Portions of the *Atocha's* hull remained intact! The study of the galleon's construction is helping us fill a large void in our knowledge of European ship-building techniques in the early seventeenth century.

SEÑORA FLORES: As a researcher in Seville, I was able to gain valuable information about the trading routes of the Spanish Empire.

EUGENE LYON: I, too, reaped historical treasure. The cups and bowls, the chains, cannons, and navigational instruments found buried beneath the sand told us a great deal about life in the early seventeenth century.

NARRATOR: Part of the treasure that Mel Fisher recovered west of the Marquesas Keys now resides in a museum in Key West, Florida. The final financial estimate of the treasure's worth has been put at over $400 million. This was not achieved without sacrifice. Four people died during the search: a visitor to the salvage operation who fell overboard, a diver named Rick Gage, and Mel's son and his wife, Dirk and Angel Fisher, who drowned when their boat capsized in the middle of the night.

MEL FISHER: Some people say that buried treasure is cursed. I have never felt that way, even after I lost my son and daughter-in-law. There is great risk in hunting treasure, and as I've said before, treasure is worth what a person is willing to pay for it. Have I paid too much? I ask myself that question every day.

SEÑORA FLORES: I read in Seville that when the *Margarita* went down in 1622, Francisco Melián, the man chosen by the crown to recover the treasure, told his crew that the first man to find the wreck would be rewarded. A slave named Juan Bañon was lucky enough to find the first ingot in that silvery cargo, and for his success, he was given his freedom. For Juan Bañon, what was the treasure truly worth?

EUGENE LYON: Treasure means different things to different people. I have spent a lifetime studying old nautical records and Spanish colonial history. For me, treasure is knowledge. The culture of Spain, its language and customs, changed half of the Western Hemisphere. Nearly four hundred years later, we are still enjoying the rich rewards of Hispanic traditions. Are cultures and history the ultimate treasure? You can exhaust a fortune. You can never exhaust the past.

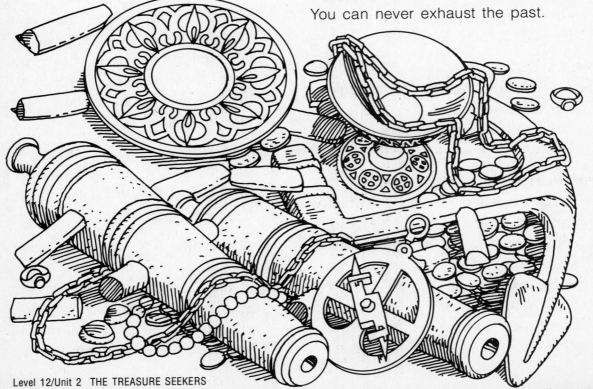

Macmillan/McGraw-Hill

Blocking Diagram

Arrange thirteen chairs, as shown. The narrator can use a music stand to hold the script.

1. NARRATOR
2. DON ANTONIO
3. CAPTAIN 1 (*Margarita*)
4. PILOT
5. ANGELES FLORES DE RODRIGUÉZ
6. EUGENE LYON
7. MEL FISHER
8. ANDRÉS LORENZO
9. CAPTAIN 2 (*Atocha*)
10. SAILOR ON THE *Atocha*
11. SILVER MASTER
12. DEO FISHER
13. DIRK FISHER
14. OPERATOR

Costume Suggestion

Don Antonio The soldier can wear a dark, long-sleeved shirt, dark pants bloused at the knee and tucked into dark knee socks, a leather breastplate, and a helmet. To make the breastplate, cut armholes and an opening for the head in a large, brown grocery bag. Then slit the bag up the back. An armor design can be created with a felt-tipped marking pen on the bag. To make a Spanish helmet, cut a crest and a brim from cardboard and tape them to a baseball cap. Then cover the headgear with aluminum foil.

Captains of the Margarita and the Atocha, the Pilot, and the Silver Master The ship captains can wear white shirts with colorful sashes draped over a shoulder and tied at the waist. The student reading the part of the pilot can dress in a white shirt, a vest, and a broad-brimmed tropical hat. To suggest an official of some importance, the silver master can wear a heavy chain and several large rings, as well as a dark, wide-brimmed hat with a large feather. All of these characters can wear dark pants tucked into knee socks to resemble breeches.

Andrés Lorenzo and Atocha Sailor The seamen can wear light-colored T-shirts with neckerchiefs tied around their necks and light-colored pants rolled up to the knees.

Macmillan/McGraw-Hill

X Marks the Spot

On September 4, 1622—a calm and sunny day—the *Nuestra Senora de Atocha,* the *Santa Margarita*, and twenty-six other ships left Havana Harbor and sailed north to the Straits of Florida where the Gulf Stream's strong currents would propel them toward Spain. By the next morning, a hurricane had entered the Straits of Florida from the northeast. The fleet was on a collision course with destiny. In all, seven ships sank during the storm.

Early treasure hunters were able to locate some of the shipwrecks and recover a small percentage of the treasure. This reproduction of the Spanish Salvors Chart of 1623 shows the *Cabeza de los Martires* (Head of the Martyrs), so named because of the number of lives lost there. The large land mass shown is the southern tip of Florida, and the small circles represent the Florida Keys.

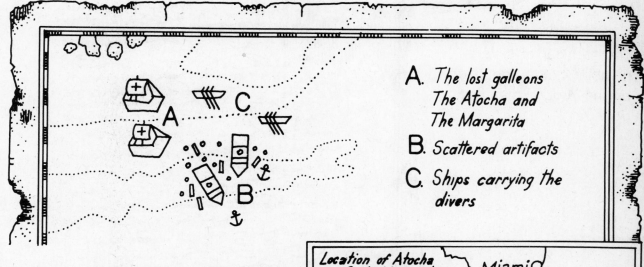

A. The lost galleons The Atocha and The Margarita

B. Scattered artifacts

C. Ships carrying the divers

By the mid-1600s, Spain had given up her attempt to recover the treasure. The precise locations of the *Atocha* and the *Margarita* were unknown until the mystery of their final resting places was finally unraveled by Mel Fisher and Eugene Lyon in 1971 and 1981. This map shows the area as we know it today.

Location of Atocha and Santa Margarita

Miami

Dry Tortugas

Marquesas Keys

Straits of Florida

CUBA

Havana

Bar Number 4,584

The first bar of silver—number 4,584—identified by the *Atocha* manifest

The *Atocha* manifest written in *procesal* script, consisted of rounded letters that were joined without punctuation. The number recorded here is *quatro mill quinientos e ochenta e quatro*. Deciphering and interpreting documents such as this manifest was Eugene Lyon's specialty.

· THE ·
TENNESSEE
TORNADO

BY SUSAN STRANE

CAST

WILMA PRESENT	WOMAN
MAMA	MAN
WILMA PAST	COACH GRAY
DOCTOR	TEAMMATE 1
MRS. HOSKINS	COACH TEMPLE
YVONNE	MAE FAGGS
TEAMMATE 2	JUDGE
TEAMMATE 3	YOUNG BOY
TEAMMATE 4	

WILMA PRESENT: I was nicknamed the "Tennessee Tornado" by the press, but my friends and family back in my hometown of Clarksville, Tennessee, knew me as just plain Wilma Rudolph. There were twenty-two kids in my family, and I was number twenty. My daddy, Ed Rudolph, worked as a railroad porter. In his spare time, he did odd jobs for people around town. My mama, whose name was Blanche, cleaned houses to make extra money. Both of them worked hard to support our large family; still, when I think back on it, we had very little money. There were lots of things we did without, but one thing we did have plenty of was love. Born on June 23, 1940, I was a premature baby, tipping the scales at just four and a half pounds. Maybe that was why I was always sick when I was growing up.

MAMA: Wilma, honey, sometimes I think you've had more than your fair share of being sick. Why, you're only three years old, and you've already had the measles, the chicken pox, the mumps, and I don't know how many colds!

WILMA PAST: Does that mean I'm special, Mama?

MAMA: Maybe it does, child. Here, now drink this down.

WILMA PAST: Oh, Mama, do I have to? I hate that stuff!

MAMA: Do you want to get well?

WILMA PAST: Yes!

MAMA: Then drink it and get under those covers. Go on now; swallow every last drop!

WILMA PRESENT: In spite of my mother's concoctions, I never had the strength that other kids had. Every cold I got seemed to last for weeks, and then it would develop into something else. When I was four, I had double pneumonia complicated by scarlet fever. That was one time Mama put her home remedies aside and called the doctor.

MAMA: She'll be all right, won't she, Doctor?

DOCTOR: She'll recover from the pneumonia and the scarlet fever, Mrs. Rudolph. But I'm afraid she contracted polio while she was ill. As a result, one of her legs is partially paralyzed. I'm sorry to have to tell you this, but I doubt that she'll ever walk again.

WILMA PAST: I *will* walk again. I will! I will!

MAMA: Yes, you will, child. We're going to fight this thing, you understand? Don't you worry, everything is going to turn out all right.

WILMA PRESENT: I started wearing a heavy metal brace to keep my leg straight. The brace went on as soon as I got up, and I wasn't allowed to take it off until I went to bed. When I was six, my mother and I started going to a hospital in Nashville for physical therapy. Twice each week, month after month, year after year—for four long years—I went for treatments. It was fifty miles each way in the back of a bus, which was the only place black people were allowed to sit. Back then, in the 1940s, there was still segregation in the South.

MAMA: There's only one seat left. You sit down, Wilma.

WILMA PAST: There are seats up front, Mama. It's not fair that you have to stand.

MAMA: No, it's not fair, and it's not right. Maybe someday things will be different. But until that time, you just hold up your head and don't let anybody get you down.

WILMA PRESENT: The treatments to strengthen my leg were painful. But even so, I looked forward to those trips to Nashville. I was getting out of Clarksville, seeing new things.

WILMA PAST: I like traveling, Mama. Someday, I'm going to break out of this brace, and I'm going to see lots of new places.

WILMA PRESENT: I guess I had big dreams even then. Sometimes after one of these trips, I would inspect my leg to see if I could detect any change. For a long time, I didn't notice any improvement.

WILMA PAST: You've just got to be better by now, leg. That doctor works on you twice every week, and Mama massages you every night. There's got to be more to life than this. You hear me? Enough is enough!

WILMA PRESENT: Yes, I started to get angry. I began to fight back in a new way. It was almost like a competition—me against my illness—and I was determined to win, no matter what!

WILMA PAST: Mama, I'm seven years old now, and I can walk pretty well with my brace. You know how you and Daddy always say education is the most important thing? Well, I'm tired of being taught at home. I want to go to school with the other kids.

MAMA: Wilma, honey, I know you've been dreaming about it for a long time. And goodness knows you've got a strong will.

WILMA PAST: Same as you do, Mama!

MAMA: Well, we'll try it out.

WILMA PRESENT: I started school as a second grader. Despite all my brave talk, I must admit I felt terrified the first day I set foot in that school. Fortunately, my teacher was a warm, supportive person who sensed that I desperately needed to belong. She was in charge of the Brownies, and she urged me to join. That turned my life around. Fourth grade was another important year for me. I had a teacher named Mrs. Hoskins. My, she was strict! But she taught me how to think positively, and I grew to love her.

MRS. HOSKINS: Wilma! How are you going to learn anything if you don't pay attention? Save your dreaming for when you sleep!

WILMA PAST: Sorry, Mrs. Hoskins, I was just looking at Nancy's picture. I sure wish I could draw as pretty as that.

MRS. HOSKINS: Wilma, if you want to do something, do it. Don't daydream about it. *Do it!*

WILMA PRESENT: By the time I was ten, everyone in town was used to seeing me with that brace. To them, it was a part of me. But not to me. One Sunday, we all went to church, like always. But it was a day I'll never forget.

MAMA: Hurry along, now. Looks like everyone is already here, except us.

WILMA PAST: You all go ahead in. I'll be along in a minute.

YVONNE: Come on, Mama. The service is about to begin.

WILMA PRESENT: I waited a few minutes before I finally went in. I knew right away that people were staring at me. I could hear them buzzing as I walked down the aisle to where my family was sitting.

WOMAN: I do declare!

MAN: I can't believe what my eyes are seeing!

WOMAN: Just look at that!

YVONNE: Mama! Daddy! It's Wilma!

MAMA: Praise be! Wilma's walking down the aisle on her own two legs. Oh, happy, happy day!

WILMA PRESENT: I had walked in without the brace. After church, a lot of people came over to congratulate me.

MAN: That's tremendous, Wilma! You sure gave us a surprise!

YVONNE: You said you'd walk again, and you did it!

WILMA PRESENT: I just smiled and beamed and didn't say much. But looking back on it, I'd say it was one of the most important moments of my life. Over the next two years, I wore the brace off and on as I regained the full use of my leg. Then, when I was in the sixth grade, Mama packed up the brace and sent it back to the hospital. Now that I had achieved my first goal, I set a new one for myself. I was determined to become someone special. That fall, I entered seventh grade, which turned out to be another pivotal year in my life.

YVONNE: Wilma, it's hard for me to believe that you'll be going to Burt High School with me this fall!

WILMA PRESENT: For the kids I knew, everything revolved around Burt High School, where Clarksville's black students attended from seventh through twelfth grades. Athletics were very important in the school, and most kids went out for a sport. My sister Yvonne was on the girls' basketball team, and I made up my mind to follow in her footsteps.

WILMA PAST: Yvonne, do you think Coach Gray will give me a chance to play on the basketball team?

YVONNE: Wilma, what are you talking about? You don't know the first thing about basketball!

WILMA PAST: That's what you think! I've been watching all of you play for years. I've studied every move. I know which ones work and which ones don't. And I'm getting real tall. What do you say, Mama?

MAMA: Child, I'm not sure if you should go out for sports. What if you fall and get hurt? I can't bear to think of all those years of massage and therapy wasted.

WILMA PAST: I'll be okay, Mama. I know I can do it!

MAMA: Well, I guess there's no use trying to change your mind. Once you get set on something, there's no stopping you.

WILMA PRESENT: I made the team, but thinking back on it, I'm fairly sure that Coach Clinton Gray selected me because of my sister. I didn't play one single minute of a game that entire season—I was a real "bench-warmer," you might say. However, I wasn't wasting time. I watched and studied everything that happened on the court. I practiced every spare minute.

MAMA: Where you going, Wilma? It's almost dinner time.

WILMA PAST: I'm just going out in the yard, Mama. I want to shoot some baskets. When Coach Gray puts me in a game, I've got to be ready, don't I?

MAMA: I never did see anyone work so hard at a thing as you do, child.

WILMA PRESENT: My mother was right. I practiced until I was shooting and rebounding better than most of my teammates. But even after three straight years, I never really got to show what I could do. Oh, I did get into some games, but only when there were a few seconds left, and the team was either way ahead or behind. I didn't complain, but sitting on the bench was getting harder and harder! At the end of my ninth-grade season, Coach Gray proposed a new idea to the team, but to our surprise, it had nothing to do with basketball.

COACH GRAY: Listen up, girls! I'm thinking of starting a girls' track team. It'll help you stay in shape for basketball. Would any of you like to go out for it?

WILMA PAST: Sure, Coach!

TEAMMATE 1: Sounds good to me!

COACH GRAY: Okay, we start on Monday.

WILMA PRESENT: I figured track would give me something to do after school between basketball seasons. As it turned out, running was pure enjoyment for me. I had no knowledge about the technical aspects of the sport or even about the work involved. But I was fast, and I won about twenty races that spring without any effort on my part. At that point, my sister gave me some friendly advice.

YVONNE: Gee, Wilma, maybe you ought to spend more time on running than on basketball. You ought to go with your strongest sport.

WILMA PAST: I love running, Yvonne, but it's just something to do in the spring. Basketball is still my favorite sport.

WILMA PRESENT: When basketball season started in my sophomore year, I felt my time had come.

WILMA PAST: Coach, I've been warming the bench for three seasons. I know I'm ready for a spot in the starting lineup. How about it?

COACH GRAY: Wilma, you're more annoying than a "skeeter" buzzing 'round my head, but you've worked real hard. All right, I'll give you a try.

WILMA PAST: Thanks, Coach. You won't be sorry!

WILMA PRESENT: Coach Gray made me a starting player—finally! The nickname that he gave me, "Skeeter," slang for mosquito, also stuck. I'll never forget my very best game that season. I scored thirty-two points and didn't miss a single shot or free throw.

COACH GRAY: You keep that up, Skeeter, and we'll make the championships this year.

WILMA PRESENT: Coach Gray's prediction was right. Our team did make it into the Tennessee High School Girls' Championships. We won a tough game in our first round, but then our smugness got the better of us. We were defeated by eight points in a game marked by sloppy ball handling and poor defense. After the game, I was crushed. Little did I know that it would turn out to be one of the most significant experiences of my entire life.

COACH TEMPLE: Excuse me, Wilma. I'd like to talk to you for a minute or two. My name's Ed Temple. I'm the coach for the Tigerbelles, the women's track team at Tennessee State University in Nashville.

WILMA PAST: Yes, sir. Say, weren't you one of the referees tonight?

COACH TEMPLE: Yes, I was. I do a lot of officiating so I can scout out new talent for my Tigerbelles. Based on what I saw tonight, I'd say you're definitely a new talent.

WILMA PAST: Thank you, Mr. Temple, but I don't know how anyone could think that after the way I played tonight!

COACH TEMPLE: Actually, Wilma, I'm thinking of another sport. With your height and long legs, you've got the makings of a sprinter. Have you ever considered competitive track?

WILMA PAST: Not really, sir. I do a lot of running after basketball season is over, but we don't have a real track team at Burt High. We don't even have a track. We jog outside and, when it rains, we run through the school.

COACH TEMPLE: Well, I know I can make a runner out of you. Just keep in mind what I've said, and we'll talk again sometime.

WILMA PRESENT: So there I was in 1956—a fifteen-year-old high school sophomore with a life that revolved around basketball, running, and my family. I'd never been so happy. As soon as basketball season ended, I put on my track shoes and started running. I ran every minute I could. I'd gotten the taste of winning and found I liked it.

COACH GRAY: Well, girls, next week is the big track meet at Tuskegee, Alabama.

WILMA PAST: Who's gonna be there, Coach?

COACH GRAY: You'll be competing against girls from all over the South. Only the best runners are invited.

TEAMMATE 1: Wow! That must mean we're pretty good.

COACH GRAY: You are, but I'd be kidding you if I didn't tell you that the competition is going to be tough, especially the girls from Atlanta, Georgia. They can practice all year round because of the warm climate there.

WILMA PAST: Don't worry, Coach. We'll make you proud of us!

WILMA PRESENT: When we got to the track, I saw that Coach Gray was right. The girls from Georgia really looked like runners. But I didn't pay much attention to them because, after my string of wins around Clarksville, I was feeling pretty cocky.

WILMA PAST: I think I can beat them. After all, I've won every single race I've ever been in.

TEAMMATE 1: I'll see you after the meet, Wilma. We're planning a big victory celebration.

WILMA PRESENT: So what happened? I didn't win a single race! I was totally devastated. My speed was no match for the training and experience of the other girls entered in the meet. I went home and moped around. Then somewhere along the line, I realized that I had learned a very important lesson: Nobody goes through life undefeated. If you can pick up after a crushing defeat and go on to win again, you're going to be a champion someday. But if losing destroys you, it's all over.

WILMA PAST: I've got to try to put it all back together. There's a lot more to track than running fast. I've got to learn the right way to run.

WILMA PRESENT: I acquired this sense of determination that I would never, ever give up no matter what else happened. I won the rest of the races I was entered in that season, but I never forgot Tuskegee. In fact, I remember thinking that anybody who had seen me lose so badly at that meet would have written me off. To my surprise, I was wrong.

COACH GRAY: Wilma, remember Ed Temple, the referee who's the women's track coach at Tennessee State? He's planning to come to Clarksville to talk with your folks.

WILMA PAST: He is? What about?

Macmillan/McGraw-Hill

COACH GRAY: I think he wants you to spend the summer at the university, learning some running techniques.

WILMA PRESENT: I rushed home to tell my mama and daddy.

MAMA: Wilma, honey, you're too young to be leaving home.

WILMA PAST: Mama, don't you see what a big break this is? If Coach Temple thinks I'm good enough, he might offer me a scholarship to the university. I could go to college!

WILMA PRESENT: While my parents talked it over with Coach Temple, I just sat tight and held my breath.

MAMA: Well, Wilma, you're the first one in this family who's ever had the chance to go to college. If running is going to do that, we just want you to put your mind to being the best you can be!

WILMA PRESENT: That summer of 1956 was no vacation for me. I learned that raw speed was not enough to win races. Coach Temple taught me breathing techniques, race strategies, and how to blast out of the starting blocks. It was hard work all right, but the hardest lesson of all was learning mental toughness.

COACH TEMPLE: Wilma, you're holding back when you run. I can see it.

WILMA PAST: Gee, Coach, I'm just a high school kid. Those girls on the senior team are older. Some of them are real track stars. I feel it would be disrespectful, almost, if I beat them.

COACH TEMPLE: Listen, Wilma, a track meet is not a popularity contest. Remember that! You're out there to win. So push for it!

WILMA PAST: I'll try, Coach.

COACH TEMPLE: You've got to do more than try, Wilma. You've got to change your mental attitude. I want you ready for the Amateur Athletic Union meet in Philadelphia, and that's only a few weeks away.

WILMA PAST: Coach, I'll be ready! I wouldn't miss it for anything. I've always dreamed of traveling.

WILMA PRESENT: We drove up to Philadelphia in a caravan of station wagons. I'd never been up North before. Everything in Philadelphia seemed so foreign to me. When we went to Franklin Stadium, I nearly fainted I was so intimidated.

WILMA PAST: I've never seen a stadium this big! I feel like a midget.

COACH TEMPLE: At six feet, you're some midget, Wilma!

WILMA PRESENT: The weeks of intensive training paid off. I won nine races, and our relay team captured the junior title.

COACH TEMPLE: You're coming along real well, Wilma. You've got a lot of potential.

WILMA PRESENT: Right after the AAU meet in Philadelphia, Coach Temple and I had a long talk.

COACH TEMPLE: You have a good possibility of making the women's Olympic track team this fall, Wilma. I think you should give it a try.

WILMA PAST: That's a pretty big track meet, isn't it, Coach?

COACH TEMPLE: It's more than a track meet. The Olympics are the oldest competitive games in the world. They were first held in Greece around 3,000 years ago. Every four years, the best amateur athletes from all over the world are chosen to compete.

WILMA PAST: Did you say that athletes come from all over the world?

COACH TEMPLE: That's right. This year the games will be held in Melbourne, Australia. You're just sixteen, but you might make it . . . if you push hard enough.

WILMA PAST: After Philadelphia, I feel I can do anything!

WILMA PRESENT: We started the first leg of our journey to Melbourne a couple of weeks later. Coach Temple drove me and a group of Tigerbelles to the Olympic tryouts in Seattle, Washington. One of these college stars was a woman named Mae Faggs. Mae held all sorts of records in women's track, and she had won medals in previous Olympics. She took a special interest in me from the first day we met.

MAE: Wilma, I'm going to give you some tough advice. Stop trying to fit in with everybody else. Stop worrying if someone is going to like you or not if you win. Start running like an individual.

WILMA PAST: I'm just a high school kid. I don't want to cause any hard feelings.

WILMA PRESENT: But Mae wasn't about to let up. When the time came for the final qualifying heat in the 200-meter dash, she took me aside.

MAE: Listen, Wilma, do you want to make the United States Olympic team?

WILMA PAST: You bet I do!

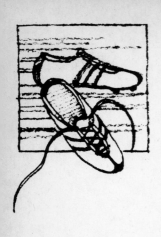

MAE: Then listen to me. All you have to do in this race is stick with me. Put everything else out of your mind.

WILMA PRESENT: I remember the gun going off, and I remember taking off with a good start. When I looked up, I saw that I had actually passed Mae and was ahead of her! She pulled up, and we finished in a dead heat, breaking the tape at the same instant!

WILMA PAST: We did it! We did it!

MAE: We sure did! We're going to the Olympics! You know, Wilma, if you hadn't pulled back, you'd have beaten me in that race. I knew you had it in you, but I wondered when it would come out. Today it did.

WILMA PAST: I don't think I'll ever be afraid to challenge anyone again. Thanks, Mae.

WILMA PRESENT: When we got back to Tennessee State, people kept coming around to wish me well.

TEAMMATE 2: Congratulations, Wilma! We're all real proud of you!

TEAMMATE 3: Hey, Wilma, you sure put Tennessee State on the map!

TEAMMATE 4: Just wait till the Olympics. Then the whole world will know about it!

WILMA PRESENT: Back home in Clarksville, everyone was excited, too.

YVONNE: Wilma, you're famous! The newspaper says you're one of the fastest women in the whole world.

MAMA: I can't help remembering, child, that only a couple of years ago, you were going to Nashville for treatments on your leg. Now here you are going to Australia for the Olympics!

MAN: We sure are proud of you, Wilma. And we want you to go to Melbourne in style, so some of the merchants in Clarksville got together to get you this luggage and a new wardrobe to take along with our very best wishes.

WILMA PAST: Thank you all, very much. I'll never forget what you've done for me.

WILMA PRESENT: In October 1956, we flew to Melbourne, Australia. At first, I felt overwhelmed by all the people speaking different languages, but I soon realized we were all there for the same reason.

WILMA PAST: You know something, Mae? For the first time in my life, I feel I'm not being judged by the color of my skin. Here, judgments depend on performance.

MAE: Well, speaking of performance, we've got to start working on ours, especially our baton-passing. There's no question about it, our timing is off.

WILMA PRESENT: Passing the baton is one of the most important and most difficult things in running a relay. Split-second timing is an absolute necessity. In fact, a number of upsets have occurred in previous Olympic Games because of an error made during a handoff.

WILMA PAST: I sure do miss Coach Temple. He'd know what we're doing wrong.

MAE: Well, we'll just have to try to remember what he taught us and keep on practicing.

WILMA PRESENT: My very first Olympic race was three days into the games. It was the qualifying heat for the 200-meter race. I made it through the first heat, and moved on to the semi-finals where only the first- and second-place runners would advance. I came in third and was eliminated. I don't know what happened, except that I didn't run as fast as I should have. I felt terrible.

WILMA PAST: I can't eat or sleep. I've let everybody down. How will I ever be able to face them back home? I'm a failure.

MAE: I know how bad you feel, Wilma, but you've got another chance to show what you can do.

WILMA PAST: You're right, Mae. I've just got to do well in the relay.

WILMA PRESENT: Before the relay, Mae, as team captain, gathered us together to give us a pep talk.

MAE: Girls, I know we can do it if we give it all we've got! Let's make it into the top three and win ourselves a medal!

WILMA PAST: We've got to—for Coach Temple and everyone else back home.

WILMA PRESENT: There were teams from six countries in that relay race, and I must confess that no one was expecting much from us. Mae ran an excellent first leg keeping us tied for the lead. The second runner lost some ground to several teams before passing the baton to me. It was a clean pass and I got off well. I passed two runners on my leg, pulling us into third place. Our anchor runner held our position. We had done it! We had captured third place and bronze medals for ourselves and for the United States.

MAE: Well, I think we can go home feeling mighty proud!

TEAMMATE 3: We sure surprised a lot of people today.

WILMA PRESENT: I was happy that I had salvaged something out of Melbourne, and I told myself a bronze medal wasn't all that bad for a sixteen-year-old from Tennessee. But as the Olympic Games ended, I could hear the voice of Mrs. Hoskins, my fourth-grade teacher.

MRS. HOSKINS: Wilma, if you want to do something, do it. Don't daydream about it. *Do it!*

WILMA PRESENT: Right then and there, I made a promise to myself.

WILMA PAST: Four years from now, wherever the Olympics are held, I'm going to be there, and I'm going to win a gold medal or two for the United States!

WILMA PRESENT: When I got home to Clarksville, I found Burt High School closed for the day so the students could attend a special assembly in my honor. When I walked out on stage, all the kids cheered and gave me flowers. After the assembly, I couldn't wait to see Coach Gray.

COACH GRAY: Congratulations, Wilma! You've come a long way. How do you feel?

WILMA PAST: Okay, but having to give that speech in the assembly scared me more than the Olympics! By the way, Coach, I heard there's a game tonight. I haven't played much basketball lately, but I'm in great shape. Can I play? Please?

COACH GRAY: Skeeter, you haven't changed a bit! Of course you can play!

WILMA PRESENT: A lot happened over the next few years. After high school, I entered Tennessee State University on a full athletic scholarship and joined Coach Temple's Tigerbelle track team. The 1960 Olympic trials were held the end of my sophomore year.

COACH TEMPLE: Are you all set Wilma? The 200-meter race is next.

WILMA PAST: I don't feel much like running today, Coach. But I'm ready to give it a try . . . and get it over with.

WILMA PRESENT: I remember when the race was over, I plopped down next to Coach Temple, and he was smiling.

COACH TEMPLE: Good race, Wilma. You're doing all right, aren't you?

WILMA PRESENT: Later, two of my teammates came running over.

TEAMMATE 2: Say, Wilma, why aren't you celebrating?

WILMA PAST: Celebrating? What for? I mean, I'm glad I made the Olympic team, but I made it once before, you know.

TEAMMATE 3: No, no, that's not what we mean. We're talking about your time—twenty-two point nine seconds.

TEAMMATE 2: It's a world record!

WILMA PAST: WHAT?

TEAMMATE 3: You mean nobody told you? You just set a record for the fastest 200 meters ever run by a woman!

WILMA PRESENT: I couldn't get over it, I'd set a world record, and I hadn't even felt like running! By the end of the trials, I'd qualified for three events—the 100 meters, the 200 meters, and the relay. Some of the other Tennessee State Tigerbelles also made the team. Best of all, Ed Temple was named coach of the United States Olympic Women's Track Team. After a three-week training session, we were off to Rome, Italy!

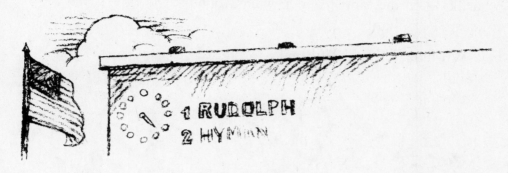

WILMA PAST: Coach Temple, I just love Rome, and this 100 degree temperature is perfect for me. It feels just like the weather in Tennessee.

COACH TEMPLE: You know, Wilma, it's a funny thing, but for the last two nights I've had the same dream. I keep seeing you with three Olympic gold medals around your neck.

WILMA PAST: I sure do hope your dream comes true!

WILMA PRESENT: But on the day before I was scheduled to run in my first race, disaster struck. It was a hot afternoon, and some of us were running through a sprinkler on a field of nice, soft grass.

TEAMMATE 2: This is a great way to cool off, isn't it?

TEAMMATE 3: Sure is, but we'd better get going. Practice starts in ten minutes, and you know how Coach Temple feels if anyone's late.

WILMA PAST: Okay. Just let me run through one last time. . . . Ow!

TEAMMATE 4: Wilma! What happened?

WILMA PAST: My ankle . . . I stepped in a hole and twisted my ankle. Ow! It hurts so much!

WILMA PRESENT: The trainer took one look and made a face; my ankle was swollen and discolored. He taped it up real tight and had me elevate it. I kept my leg up until the next morning—the day of the 100-meter final. Rumors were flying that I was out of the race. But when I put my weight on my foot, my ankle held up. I knew then I'd be able to run. That day, the stadium was jammed. For some reason, the fans had taken a liking to me, and when I walked out on the track, they started to chant.

ALL: Wil-ma! Wil-ma! Wil-ma!

WILMA PRESENT: The tension was building. I put everything out of my mind and concentrated on the race I had to run. Then we were off! My start was good; I came out second or third in the field. My ankle felt all right. When I reached fifty meters, I saw that I had left them all behind—and I was just beginning to turn on the speed. By seventy meters, I knew the race was mine; nobody was going to catch me. I had won my first gold medal!

COACH TEMPLE: That's number one, Wilma!

WILMA PAST: Three days later, I ran in the 200-meter final.

ALL: Wil-ma! Wil-ma! Wil-ma! Go . . . go . . . go!

COACH TEMPLE: She's way ahead. She's going to do it!

TEAMMATE 3: Wilma did it again! She's got her second gold!

WILMA PRESENT: That left the relay. This was my chance to become the first American woman to win three Olympic gold medals. Everybody was talking about the teams from Russia, West Germany, and Britain. Well, we beat them *and* set a world's record in the process! The crowd went wild.

ALL: Wil-ma! Wil-ma! Hooray!

WILMA PRESENT: I had done it—the first American woman to win three gold medals. I had to share the moment with my family.

WILMA PAST:

Dear Folks,
 Three Olympic gold medals — what a feeling! After the playing of "The Star Spangled Banner," I came away from the victory stand, and I was mobbed. People were pushing microphones into my face, pounding my back, and calling me the "Tennessee Tornado." I couldn't believe it. Finally, the American officials grabbed me and escorted me to safety. One of them told me that life would never be the same again.

RUDOLPH WINS GOLD!

WILMA PRESENT: That official was right! I was the darling of the press, but some animosity was developing toward me on the part of the other American women runners. The jealousy grew so intense that some of the Tigerbelles—girls I had been running with for years—were turning on me.

TEAMMATE 2: Listen to this. The paper says she has long, lissome legs and a pert charm.

TEAMMATE 3: How nice.

TEAMMATE 2: There's more. It says she makes all the other runners look like they're churning on a treadmill.

TEAMMATE 4: That means us, right?

TEAMMATE 2: No one talks about *us*. It's just Wilma, Wilma, Wilma. They forget that we ran the relay, too.

WILMA PRESENT: It all came to a head—literally—in London, where our team was participating in the British Empire Games. I had to appear at a banquet, and I looked a mess.

WILMA PAST: Oh, where are those hair rollers? I've got to meet Coach Temple in an hour and I look awful.

TEAMMATE 2: Gee, Wilma, I have no idea where they are.

TEAMMATE 4: Me, either.

TEAMMATE 3: Don't worry, Wilma. I'm sure they'll love you anyway.

WILMA PRESENT: When Coach Temple learned what had happened, he was furious. He called a team meeting, but as he discovered the next day, his lecture didn't have much effect. The Tigerbelles were entered in the women's relay. The stadium was packed with fans who wanted to see the fastest women's relay team in history, but my three teammates had something else in mind.

TEAMMATE 2: Let's just take it easy today, ladies.

TEAMMATE 3: Yeah! I'm feeling kinda tired.

WILMA PRESENT: They loped around the track just fast enough to keep us in the race. By the time I got the baton, the leading runner was forty yards ahead of me. Well, I was determined to win that race, so I poured on the speed. I caught up with the front runner at the tape—and won! The crowd went wild. So did Coach Temple.

COACH TEMPLE: When we get back to Tennessee State, you three are on probation!

WILMA PRESENT: From that point on, my teammates ran their best, but they shunned me when we were off the field. It was a relief when Coach Temple announced that we were going home. We landed at the Nashville airport, and home had never looked so good.

WILMA PAST: I never expected such a huge crowd, Coach.

COACH TEMPLE: Seems like everyone in Nashville is here to greet us—the governor, the mayor, television stations, marching bands. I've never seen anything like it.

WILMA PAST: It's great, Coach, but I just want to go home to my family in Clarksville.

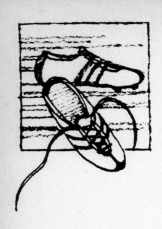

WILMA PRESENT: In a few days, my folks joined me in a motorcade parade down the streets of my hometown. It was the most amazing event because the whole town—black and white—turned out to greet me.

WILMA PAST: Mama, do you realize this parade is the very first integrated event in Clarksville?

MAMA: And you made it happen, Wilma. Why, I never thought I'd live to see this day.

WILMA PRESENT: That night, for the first time in the history of Clarksville, black people and white people attended a banquet together. One of the featured speakers was County Judge William Hudson.

Macmillan/McGraw-Hill

JUDGE: Welcome, everyone. Wilma Rudolph has competed with the world and has brought home three gold medals. Not only that, she has inspired another victory right here at home. In working together to put on this banquet in her honor, I think we've learned a worthwhile lesson: If you want to get good music out of a piano, you have to play both the white and the black keys.

WILMA PRESENT: By the beginning of 1961, I'd completed my education, getting a degree in elementary education. I'd also received hundreds of invitations and honors. One of my proudest moments came when President Kennedy invited me, my mother, and Coach Temple to the White House. After returning from that Washington trip, I started to do some hard thinking.

WILMA PAST: I'm twenty-two years old, and I've won three Olympic gold medals. So where do I go from here, Coach?

COACH TEMPLE: What about the 1964 Olympics, Wilma?

WILMA PAST: I don't know. . . . I want to have a family, and I'd like to help kids like me make it. On the other hand, it would be exciting to compete again in '64. But if I did, I'd have to win at least three more gold medals, or else people would think I'm a failure.

COACH TEMPLE: I understand, Wilma, and remember this: If you lose in '64, that's what people will remember—the losses, not the three gold medals in 1960.

WILMA PRESENT: I had a lot to think about. Then, in 1962, a major meet was slated with the Soviet Union. I trained hard, for in the back of my mind was the thought that this might be the right time to end my career. I wanted to retire on top, even if it meant retiring earlier than I needed to. First came the 100 meters, and I won it easily. Then came the relay, an event the Russian team excelled at. When I got the baton for the final lap, the Russian runner was about forty yards ahead of me. I started picking up speed and closing on her.

COACH TEMPLE: That's the way, Wilma! Pour it on!

WILMA PRESENT: She saw me coming out of the corner of her eye, and I could tell she couldn't believe that I was there. Well, I caught her, passed her, and won the race. The crowd was on its feet, giving me a standing ovation, and I knew that it was time—time to retire, with the sweet taste of victory.

WILMA PAST: Whew! I thought I'd never finish signing autographs. I know I'll miss the running, but this day had to come sometime, didn't it, Coach?

COACH TEMPLE: It comes to all of us. You're a real champ, Wilma. You've opened lots of doors for lots of people. I'll always be proud of you. Are you okay? Do you want a lift back to the hotel?

WILMA PAST: I think I'd just like to sit here by myself for awhile. Thanks for everything, Coach.

WILMA PRESENT: I was untying my track shoes, when out from the shadows came a young boy who had been pushed aside by the crowd. He was clutching a scrap of paper and a pencil.

YOUNG BOY: Miss Rudolph . . . ?

WILMA PAST: Have you been waiting all this time? Come on over and sit down by me. Do you want to be a runner, too?

YOUNG BOY: Yes, and I dream about being in the Olympics some day. Miss Rudolph, . . . can I please have your autograph?

WILMA PAST: Son, I'll do better than that.

WILMA PRESENT: I took off my track shoes and signed my name on both of them. Then I handed them to the boy.

WILMA PAST: Here, these are for you. And let me tell you what someone once told me: If you want to do something, do it. Don't daydream about it. *Do it!*

BLOCKING DIAGRAM

Arrange sixteen chairs, as shown. The narrator, Wilma Present, can use a music stand to hold the script.

1. WILMA PRESENT
2. DOCTOR
3. YVONNE
4. MAMA
5. WILMA PAST
6. COACH TEMPLE

7. TEAMMATE 2
8. TEAMMATE 3
9. TEAMMATE 4
10. WOMAN
11. MAN
12. MRS. HOSKINS

13. COACH GRAY
14. MAE FAGGS
15. TEAMMATE 1
16. JUDGE
17. YOUNG BOY

Macmillan/McGraw-Hill

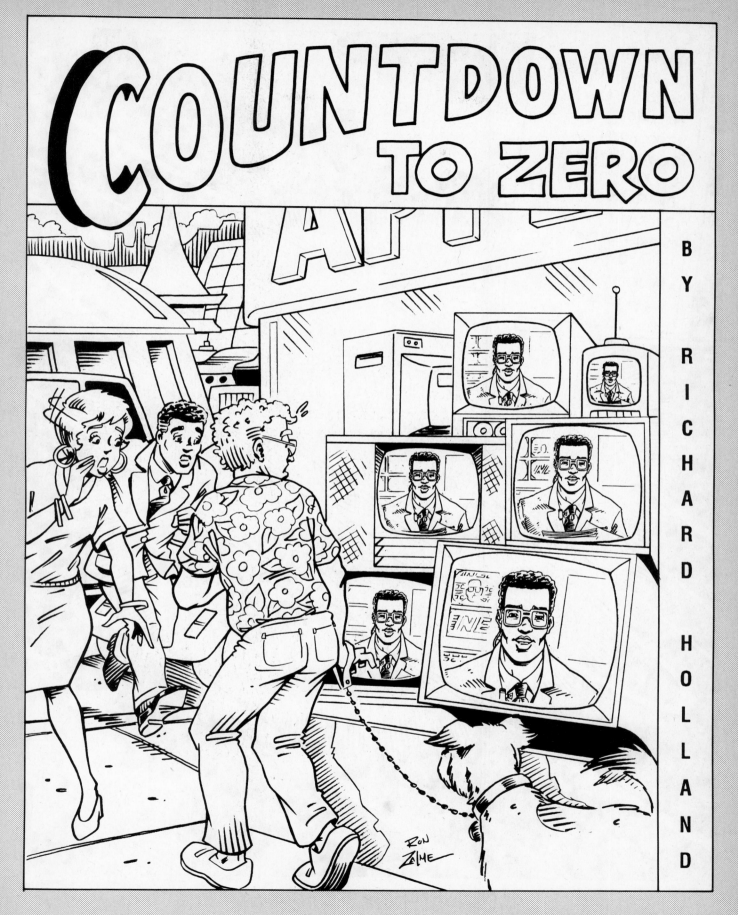

COUNTDOWN TO ZERO

BY RICHARD HOLLAND

NEWSCASTER: Good morning. It's 8 A.M., and I'm Bob Fredrickson with the Satellite News brief. First, a report from the science desk. Yesterday, in a medical breakthrough, doctors completed the first transplant of a human brain into a cyborg. The operation took thirty-two hours and was performed by three teams of surgeons. In other news, swarms of monarch butterflies, which usually migrate to Mexico at this time of year, have settled in the peach groves of Georgia. Biologists cannot explain this change in the migratory pattern of the butterflies. However, the residents of Georgia are said to be enjoying their new guests. Now, for a sports update . . .

DR. ROYAL: Sandy! Nicky! Better turn off the TV and get ready to leave for school!

SANDY: Okay, Mom. We're almost ready.

SOUND EFFECT: [*TV being switched off*]

NARRATOR: Sandy and Nicky, twelve-year-old twins of geophysicist Dr. Samantha Royal, were starting what they thought would be just another ordinary day. They had no idea that this day would mark the beginning of the most terrifying period in the earth's history.

DR. ROYAL: Here are your lunches, kids.

SOUND EFFECT: [*scratching on wood*]

DR. ROYAL: What's that scratching sound at the front door?

NICKY: I'll see.

SOUND EFFECT: [*door opening*]

NICKY: Hey, it's a cat!

SANDY: I recognize it. That's Bobby Sander's cat.

NICKY: Hmmm . . . that's funny. What's it doing way over here?

SANDY: Weird. We can drop it off at Bobby's house on our way to school.

NICKY: Hey, look at that! It looks like all the neighbors' cats are wandering up and down the street!

DR. ROYAL: That *is* strange. Well, we'd all better get going, or we'll be late.

Macmillan/McGraw-Hill

SOUND EFFECT: [*door opening and closing; car starting*]

NARRATOR: The twins went off to school, and Dr. Royal went off to her lab without another thought about butterflies or cats. Her mind was on an important experiment that she and her colleague, Dr. Art Parker, had been working on for nearly four years. Now their work had reached a crucial stage.

DR. PARKER: Samantha, I think we're pretty close to fusing hepalite and tungasium to make artificial plasmonium.

SOUND EFFECT: [*clinking and clanking of lab equipment*]

DR. ROYAL: I think you're right, Art. I just hope Centripetal Corporation comes up with the grant money we need to complete our experiments.

DR. PARKER: They have to. How else will they get a substance as heavy as plasmonium for their moon anchors? Ever since mining natural plasmonium became illegal, they've been searching for a method to produce it synthetically.

SOUND EFFECT: [*knock and door opening*]

DR. KILE: Samantha! Art! Do you have a spare minute or two? Dr. Graybar would like you to come to the conference room.

DR. ROYAL: We can always find time for Dr. Graybar! What's up, Dr. Kile?

DR. KILE: It's the monarch butterfly problem. He's looking for some answers.

DR. ROYAL: But we're geophysicists, not biologists.

DR. KILE: Exactly what he needs.

DR. ROYAL: If you say so . . .

SOUND EFFECT: [*footsteps of three people*]

NARRATOR: Dr. Royal and Dr. Parker entered the conference room and found a group of distinguished scientists assembled there.

DR. GRAYBAR: Ah, yes. Welcome Dr. Royal, Dr. Parker. I think you know everyone here. We've been discussing a very serious matter. It seems that the monarch butterfly phenomenon is a manifestation of a more complex problem. Other species of animals have been exhibiting strange behavior, as well.

DR. ROYAL: Hmmm. That's interesting. Just this morning, my family noticed that all the neighborhood cats seemed to be wandering around as if lost.

DR. GRAYBAR: Exactly! I'm convinced there is a connection between the cats and the butterflies.

DR. PARKER: Really? Could you explain? I'm afraid you've lost me!

DR. GRAYBAR: Well, we know butterflies migrate using a form of internal radar tuned to the earth's magnetic field. Cats don't migrate, of course. But cats *have* been known to find their way home from hundreds of miles away using the same type of internal detection system.

DR. PARKER: Fascinating! Do you think there's been some kind of change in the magnetic field of the earth?

DR. GRAYBAR: That may be a possibility, but we don't know for sure. Centromagnetism is your area of expertise. That's why I asked you and Dr. Royal to attend this meeting.

DR. ROYAL: It could be disastrous if the earth's magnetic field changed even to the slightest millibar.

DR. PARKER: Absolutely!

SOUND EFFECT: [*knock at the door*]

DR. ORTIZ: Dr. Graybar! Excuse me a moment, Dr. Graybar!

DR. GRAYBAR: Yes, Dr. Ortiz?

DR. ORTIZ: The National Weather Center in Washington just called. The sun . . . the sun rose forty-three point nine seconds too early this morning!

SOUND EFFECT: [*gasps from all*]

DR. GRAYBAR: This is even worse than we thought. If we don't come up with some answers quickly, I'm afraid that our planet will be facing serious consequences.

NARRATOR: The meeting concluded with an assignment of tasks. Each team of scientists began working at a frantic pace. Dr. Royal and Dr. Parker set about measuring the earth's magnetic field.

DR. ROYAL: Are the instruments set?

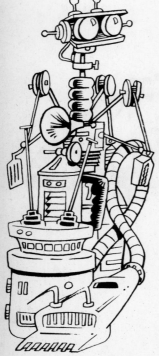

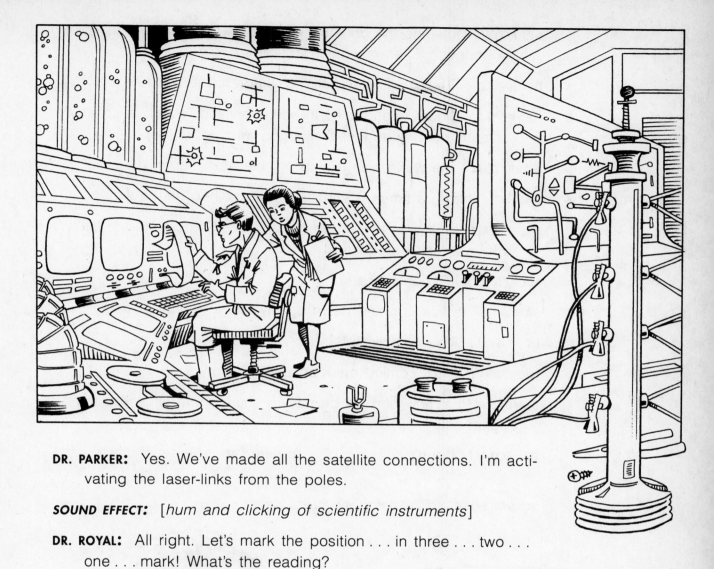

DR. PARKER: Yes. We've made all the satellite connections. I'm activating the laser-links from the poles.

SOUND EFFECT: [*hum and clicking of scientific instruments*]

DR. ROYAL: All right. Let's mark the position . . . in three . . . two . . . one . . . mark! What's the reading?

DR. PARKER: This is unbelievable!

DR. ROYAL: What is it, Art?

DR. PARKER: Magnetic north has moved three millibars to the east!

DR. ROYAL: That's impossible. Check again! Mark in three . . . two . . . one . . . mark! What's your reading now?

DR. PARKER: It's moved again! This time it's two millibars to the *west*!

DR. ROYAL: How can that be? Maybe the instruments are faulty.

DR. PARKER: No, I checked them thoroughly before we started. Samantha, there's no denying the fact that magnetic north is no longer constant! This must be why the sun has been rising at unpredictable times.

DR. ROYAL: Imagine the potential effect on weather patterns! What will happen when the polar ice caps begin to melt?

DR. PARKER: The tides will surely be affected; the seasons, too.

DR. ROYAL: Since magnetic north keeps shifting, we have no way of predicting when these changes will occur.

NARRATOR: The world was to find out the next morning.

SANDY: Mom, it's time for school, but it's still so dark out.

DR. ROYAL: Well, the sun is coming up now. Come look out the window. Isn't it beautiful?

NICKY: Look! Look at that!

SANDY: The sun is going down again—like it's setting!

DR. ROYAL: This is incredible!

NICKY: Wait. It's coming back up again!

SANDY: Mom, how can we be having sunrise and sunset at the same time?

DR. ROYAL: I don't know—yet. Let's see if there is anything on the news.

SOUND EFFECT: [*TV being switched on*]

NEWSCASTER: Here's the latest Satellite News brief. This morning, millions of people witnessed an unbelievable sight: the sun rising twice in one morning. Scientists are at a loss to explain the phenomenon.

Macmillan/McGraw-Hill

NARRATOR: Within a few minutes, the phone lines were jammed. Police departments all over the country were flooded with calls from confused and frightened residents.

SOUND EFFECT: [*phone ringing*]

SHERIFF: Hello. Yes, this is Sheriff Green. Mr. Boynton! How are you this morning? What do you mean "Which morning?" Tuesday morning, of course. No, no, it's not Wednesday. Yes, it *is* a new day each time the sun rises. Yes, the sun did rise twice today, but it's still Tuesday. At least I think it's still Tuesday. No, I don't know who to ask. Best thing to do is to stay tuned to the local news satellite.

NEWSCASTER: We interrupt this program to bring you a special Satellite News bulletin. Tidal waves as high as 120 feet are being reported from coastal communities around the world! Residents are being evacuated. Scientists believe the waves are related to the double sunrise this morning. Satellite News will continue to provide updates on events as they occur.

NARRATOR: All over the world, scientists were meeting in an attempt to analyze the situation.

SOUND EFFECT: [*hum of many voices; banging of a gavel*]

DR. GRAYBAR: Will the meeting please come to order! Please come to order! Dr. Ortiz, you have the floor.

DR. ORTIZ: This double-sunrise phenomenon must be an optical illusion. I can find no other explanation for it.

DR. ROYAL: I know that as an astronomer you find it particularly difficult to believe, Dr. Ortiz. But it is not an optical illusion. It *did* happen.

DR. KILE: What do you think is causing it, Dr. Royal?

DR. ROYAL: I can't assign causality yet, Dr. Kile. But I do believe the earth is no longer spinning in a constant motion on its axis.

SOUND EFFECT: [*hum of very excited voices; banging of a gavel*]

DR. GRAYBAR: Ladies and gentlemen, please! I am sure Dr. Royal has good reasons for making such a radical statement. I, for one, would like to hear them.

DR. ROYAL: Thank you, Dr. Graybar. According to our calculations— and I know this sounds incredible—the earth is wobbling.

DR. KILE: Wobbling? What in the world do you mean?

DR. ROYAL: Based on a series of measurements, Dr. Parker and I have discovered that the angle of the earth's tilt on its axis keeps varying. The earth is actually tilting back and forth one to three millibars every day. This means, of course, that the horizon line keeps fluctuating.

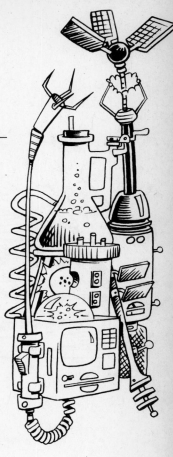

DR. PARKER: In other words, after the sun rises, the horizon moves up and covers it again, making it appear as if the sun is set- ting. When the earth tips down again, the sun appears to be rising a second time.

DR. ROYAL: We believe the unusual events that have occurred re- cently—the double sunrises, the tidal waves, the deviation in animal migratory patterns—have been caused by the earth wobbling.

DR. GRAYBAR: But *why* is the earth wobbling?

DR. ROYAL: We don't know yet. That's the next mystery to be solved.

NARRATOR: A few days later, while scouting around for rocks to in- clude in their science-fair project, Sandy and Nicky stumbled onto what turned out to be an important clue.

SOUND EFFECT: [*footsteps walking over rocks and gravel*]

NICKY: What a great place to find unusual rocks! It's almost as good as the old quarry.

SANDY: It sure is. Hey, look at that pink glow! It seems to be coming from one of the rocks over there.

NICKY: Over where?

SANDY: Near that maglev track that leads to the old abandoned mine shaft! See? Come on—that would be a great sample to have.

SOUND EFFECT: [*footsteps running over rocks and gravel*]

NICKY: I've got my collection bag ready and waiting. Just drop it in.

SANDY: I can't, Nicky. It's too heavy!

NICKY: What do you mean it's too heavy? It's as small as a marble.

SANDY: You try picking it up. It won't budge. It weighs a ton!

NICKY: Sandy, look at your hand! It's glowing pink!

SANDY: Oh, no! It must be from this rock!

NICKY: Try wiping it off on the grass!

SANDY: I am! It won't come off!

NARRATOR: Just then, the owner of the abandoned mine spotted the twins.

MINE OWNER: Hey! You kids! What are you doing? Get away from there! Don't let me catch you here again! Foster, get over here and help me move those rocks!

MINE MANAGER: Right away, boss!

NARRATOR: Terrified, the twins hurried home. Sandy tried to scrub the pink rock dust from her hand, but no matter what she used, her hand still glowed.

SOUND EFFECT: [*running water followed by opening and closing of a door*]

DR. ROYAL: Hi, I'm home!

SANDY: Mom! Mom! Look at my hand! I can't get this pink stuff off! Is it dangerous?

DR. ROYAL: Let me see it. How did this happen?

NICKY: Sandy touched a pink rock. I mean, it was glowing pink.

SANDY: Am I going to die?

DR. ROYAL: No, this is plasmonium dust. It's not toxic, and it'll wear off in a couple of days. You'll be fine, Sandy. But where on earth did you find plasmonium?

NICKY: We were near that abandoned mine looking for rocks for our science project.

DR. ROYAL: You mean the old Centripetal Corporation mine?

SANDY: Yes.

DR. ROYAL: Do you have the rock?

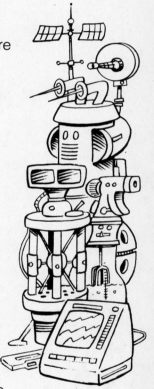

NICKY: No, it was too heavy to pick up. Besides, some men chased us away. They were really mean.

DR. ROYAL: Hmmm. There's something odd about all this. That mine has been shut down for over ten years. Listen, I don't want you two going back there. It's not a safe place.

SANDY: Okay, Mom. It *was* kind of spooky.

DR. ROYAL: Do you remember exactly where you found that rock?

NICKY: We found it right near one of the maglev tracks that comes out of the old mine shaft.

SANDY: Hold on a minute. I think I remember seeing a faded old sign that said shaft six.

DR. ROYAL: Thanks, eagle eye! I'd better call Art Parker right away.

SOUND EFFECT: [*dialing of telephone*]

DR. ROYAL: Hello, Art? Listen, I have a hunch that Centripetal Corporation is mining plasmonium again!

DR. PARKER: What makes you think so?

DR. ROYAL: Sandy and Nicky found a sample of the ore right outside Centripetal's so-called abandoned mine. Sandy's hand is still glowing pink.

DR. PARKER: Hmmm. Since the glow-life of plasmonium is eight days, that means the sample is fresh. Wasn't Centripetal mining from the earth's mantle before they were ordered to shut down?

DR. ROYAL: Yes, but they had pretty much exhausted the supply of plasmonium in the mantle. That's why they applied for a permit to mine in the earth's core.

DR. PARKER: Right, it's coming back to me now. That's when the International Earth Preservation Organization banned *all* mining of plasmonium to conserve the little that remained.

DR. ROYAL: That's correct. . . . Art, I have an idea.

DR. PARKER: What?

DR. ROYAL: Well, you know how desperate Centripetal has been for a plasmonium substitute for their moon anchors. . . .

DR. PARKER: Ye-e-s . . .

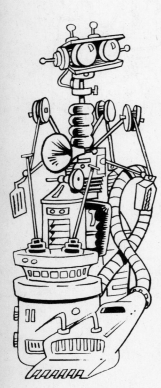

DR. ROYAL: Let's just suppose for a moment that they couldn't wait for our fusion experiments to yield results, so they started mining plasmonium from the earth's core—secretly, of course. Since plasmonium is earth's heaviest known substance, . . .

DR. PARKER: . . . if enough of it were removed from the core, it could cause the earth to become unbalanced!

DR. ROYAL: Exactly! I think we're on to something, Art. This could be . . .

SOUND EFFECT: [*loud rumble followed by crash of something heavy falling*]

SANDY: What's that?

NICKY: What's going on?

DR. ROYAL: Quick, turn on Satellite News.

SOUND EFFECT: [*TV being switched on*]

DR. PARKER: [*muffled voice*] Samantha, Samantha!

DR. ROYAL: Art, Art, are you still there? Are you all right?

DR. PARKER: Wow! Yes, I'm okay. How about you and the kids?

DR. ROYAL: We're all right, too. This is getting to be very serious. We've got to do something—fast.

DR. PARKER: You'd better report your suspicions about Centripetal Corporation to Dr. Graybar.

DR. ROYAL: I will—right away.

SOUND EFFECT: [*telephone receiver being replaced*]

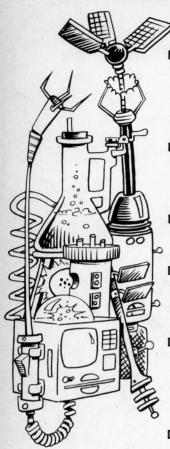

NARRATOR: Dr. Graybar was shocked by what Dr. Royal had to say. The next morning, he called an emergency meeting of the IEPO—the International Earth Preservation Organization. The member countries were immediately linked by satel-vision.

DR. PARKER: As you all know, Dr. Royal and I have concluded that the earth is wobbling because it's out of balance. Now we have a hypothesis to explain this phenomenon.

DR. ROYAL: We have reason to believe that Centripetal Corporation is mining plasmonium from the earth's core.

DR. KILE: But Centripetal's license to mine plasmonium was canceled ten years ago. You yourself were on the inspection team, Dr. Royal.

DR. ROYAL: That's true. But inspections at the mine site were stopped more than a year ago. Now, if they *have* been mining from the core in this past year, they could have removed as much as 250 trillion qwarnels of plasmonium.

DR. PARKER: This would explain why the earth is unbalanced, and why the earth's magnetic field keeps changing.

DR. ORTIZ: What evidence do you have to back up this notion?

DR. ROYAL: Yesterday my children found a small sample of plasmonium ore near Centripetal Corporation's abandoned mine.

DR. KILE: Do you have the sample?

DR. ROYAL: Regrettably, no. It was much too heavy for them to lift. And when the people from Centripetal saw the children, they chased them off.

DR. ORTIZ: Now Dr. Royal, you can't expect us to take the word of children when the future of the nation . . .

DR. KILE: The earth!

DR. GRAYBAR: The universe!

DR. ORTIZ: Yes! When the future of the entire universe is at stake.

DR. ROYAL: I myself saw the plasmonium dust on my daughter's hand. The situation is critical. According to my calculations, if the earth tilts another nine millibars, the planet will go hurtling out into space!

DR. PARKER: And it will only take the removal of another two million qwarnels of plasmonium to make that happen. So you see, Centripetal must be investigated immediately.

DR. ORTIZ: Just the same, I think we must study the problem a little while longer.

DR. KILE: I agree with Dr. Ortiz. We must not be too hasty. After all, Centripetal Corporation did give us over two hundred million dollars for scientific research last year.

DR. GRAYBAR: Dr. Royal, we need concrete evidence. It would not be responsible to accuse Centripetal without proof.

NARRATOR: Unable to convince the organization to take immediate action, Dr. Royal and Dr. Parker went back to their lab and pondered the problem.

SOUND EFFECT: [*footsteps followed by door opening and closing*]

DR. ROYAL: Art, we can't just sit by and let Centripetal Corporation destroy the entire world.

DR. PARKER: But Dr. Graybar is right. We can't accuse them of mining plasmonium without concrete evidence, Samantha.

DR. ROYAL: Then we'll have to get the evidence!

DR. PARKER: How? We can't go marching up to them and say we'd like to take a little tour of their abandoned mine.

DR. ROYAL: No, we can't. What we can do is figure out a way to get into the mine. If we find any traces of glowing plasmonium in the mine shafts, we'll have our proof.

DR. PARKER: But how will we know where to search? There are hundreds of shafts in Centripetal's mine.

DR. ROYAL: I still have a map of that mine from when I served on the inspection team. Let's go back to my house and take a look in my files.

SOUND EFFECT: [*door opening and closing; car starting*]

NARRATOR: As the two scientists headed for Dr. Royal's house, the owner of Centripetal Corporation met with the manager of the mine.

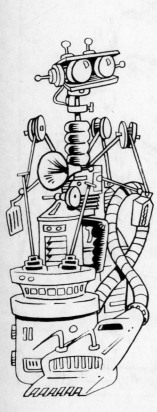

MINE MANAGER: Those kids were a little too interested in that pink rock. You know, boss, I think I recognized them. Their mother is that scientist, Samantha Royal. Remember her? She was on the inspection team that kept us shut down for ten years.

MINE OWNER: Do I ever remember! But we managed to outfox them, didn't we, Foster? We didn't do any plasmonium mining, but we kept all the *equipment* in running order. Nothing illegal about that!

MINE MANAGER: Yeah! And then when they finally decided it was safe to stop inspections after ten years, we were able to get right back in business—quietly, of course!

MINE OWNER: Right. We've been very careful. So don't worry about those kids—or their mother. They don't know anything.

MINE MANAGER: Say, boss—off the record—you don't think our mining has anything to do with this earth-wobbling thing, do you?

MINE OWNER: Nah! People have been mining for years, and the earth has never wobbled.

MINE MANAGER: But they were mining in the earth's mantle. We've gone into the core.

MINE OWNER: Don't worry, I tell you. Besides, we only need to keep going for another month or so. Another two million qwarnels of plasmonium, and we'll all be able to retire—very comfortably.

MINE MANAGER: Yeah, we'll be rich, all right. Very rich!

MINE OWNER: It probably wouldn't hurt to beef up security, just in case anyone starts to get nosy.

MINE MANAGER: Should I post a guard at the northeast end of the mine?

MINE OWNER: No, that might make it look as if we have something to hide. We can't do anything that might arouse suspicion. Let's just make sure that everything looks as if it hasn't been disturbed for the last ten years. And, for Pete's sake, check to see that there's no more plasmonium ore lying around!

NARRATOR: Meanwhile, Dr. Royal and Dr. Parker examined the company's maps and developed a plan.

SOUND EFFECT: [*crackle of paper unfolding*]

DR. ROYAL: Let's see. Sandy said she thought she found the rock that was glowing pink near shaft six.

DR. PARKER: Uh-huh. Four . . . seven . . . six! Here it is, in the northeast quadrant.

DR. ROYAL: Art, I'm fairly certain that's where Centripetal had proposed to dig into the earth's core.

DR. PARKER: Well, Samantha, I'm convinced. I'd say there isn't a minute to lose. The sooner we look into this, the better.

DR. ROYAL: It's still fairly early; how about going right now? I'll just leave a note for the kids.

SOUND EFFECT: [*start-up noise of computer followed by clicking of keyboard*]

DR. ROYAL: Let's see now . . .

Dear Sandy and Nicky,
Dr. Parker and I are going to take a look at Centripetal Corporation's mine. There's a frozen pizza and some veggies in the fridge. If I'm not back by eight o'clock, call Aunt Holly and ask her to come over. See you in the morning.

Love you,
Mom

NARRATOR: Dr. Royal left the note on the kitchen counter, where Sandy and Nicky would be sure to see it. Then she and Dr. Parker headed out to the mine.

SOUND EFFECT: [*door closing; car starting*]

Macmillan/McGraw-Hill

NARRATOR: As they drove away, Dr. Royal had no way of knowing that a sudden gust of wind caused by closing the door had blown the note off the counter. It fell to the floor and came to rest under the refrigerator.

DR. ROYAL: Let's park down the road from the mine and walk the rest of the way.

SOUND EFFECT: [*car stopping; two doors closing quietly*]

DR. PARKER: So far, so good. There doesn't seem to be anyone around.

NARRATOR: The two made their way to the northeast quadrant and found the tracks leading to shaft six. There was an old wooden door with a padlock on it blocking the entrance.

DR. PARKER: This doesn't look as if it's been used in the past ten years, let alone the past year.

DR. ROYAL: That's true. This wood is so old, it's rotting away. I wonder how sturdy it is. . . .

SOUND EFFECT: [*crack of breaking wood; creaking hinges*]

DR. PARKER: It broke right off its hinges.

DR. ROYAL: That's what you call a lucky break! And we'd might as well make the most of it.

DR. PARKER: Go ahead. I'm right behind you. Look! Shine the flashlight along the wall down there. Hmmm. There's certainly no pink glow. Just a lot of dusty rocks.

DR. ROYAL: Look here. It's the high-speed elevator they built when they applied for permission to mine the core. Come over here on the platform and take a look at the control panel. See, they installed stops down to minus twenty.

DR. PARKER: I doubt if they ever got around to wiring it up.

NARRATOR: As he spoke, Dr. Parker absentmindedly pushed one of the buttons.

SOUND EFFECT: [*click*]

DR. ROYAL: The light went on!

DR. PARKER: Let's see what happens if I press minus three.

SOUND EFFECT: [*whirring and hum of an elevator*]

DR. ROYAL: We're moving! What's going on here?

DR. PARKER: It's working—and it doesn't even squeak. Samantha, this elevator has been used very recently. I'm sure of it.

SOUND EFFECT: [*elevator hum stopping; door sliding open*]

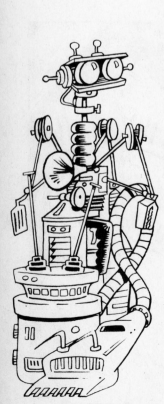

NARRATOR: At minus three, the elevator stopped and the door slid open. Suddenly, the two scientists were bathed in a glow of pink light.

DR. ROYAL: Art! This is it!

DR. PARKER: Plasmonium! Tons of it! This must be their loading dock!

NARRATOR: Dr. Royal took a microcamera out of her pocket and began filming while Dr. Parker took a tiny rock sample and put it into his backpack. They were both very conscious of the need to work quickly.

DR. ROYAL: That should do it. We've got our proof now!

DR. PARKER: Right. Let's go back up. Hurry!

SOUND EFFECT: [*hum of elevator coming to a sudden stop*]

DR. ROYAL: It stopped. How come the door isn't opening?

DR. PARKER: I don't know. Here, let's try this lever. Give me a hand.

DR. ROYAL: It won't budge. It seems to be jammed!

SOUND EFFECT: [*static*]

DR. PARKER: The lights are flickering, too! There may be a short in the wiring.

DR. ROYAL: Or maybe they turn off the power at night.

DR. PARKER: Uh-oh! *None* of the buttons are working now.

DR. ROYAL: We're stuck!

DR. PARKER: I don't see any way out of here.

DR. ROYAL: I'm afraid there's only one way. In my note, I told the twins where we were going. When they realize I'm not back, I'm sure they'll get help. There is one hitch, though.

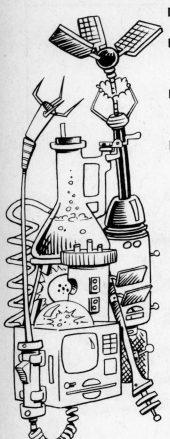

DR. PARKER: What's that?

DR. ROYAL: I said I'd see them in the morning. That's several hours from now!

DR. PARKER: Well, let's just hope there are no earth tremors between now and then.

NARRATOR: No sooner were the words out of Dr. Parker's mouth, than they heard a sound that made their blood run cold.

SOUND EFFECT: [*rumble that gets louder and louder*]

DR. PARKER: What is that?

DR. ROYAL: It sounds like the mine is collapsing!

SOUND EFFECT: [*bumping noises as elevator car shakes*]

DR. PARKER: Hang on!

NARRATOR: Meanwhile, at Samantha's house, the twins had finished their dinner and were taking a break from their homework.

SANDY: I don't understand it. Mom *always* lets us know if she's going to be home late.

NICKY: I know. I called the lab. No one answers. I tried Dr. Parker, too, but he's not home, either. I'm worried.

SANDY: Me, too. Let's check Mom's appointment book. Maybe that'll tell us something.

NARRATOR: The children went into their mother's office.

NICKY: I feel funny about this. You know we're not allowed in here when Mom's not home.

SANDY: I know, but this is special.

SOUND EFFECT: [*papers rustling*]

SANDY: Look at this!

NICKY: Hey, it's a map of the Centripetal mines.

SANDY: And someone's drawn a circle around shaft six. That's where we found the plasmonium.

NICKY: Are you thinking what I'm thinking?

SANDY: I sure am! We'd better call Sheriff Green right away.

NARRATOR: After hearing what Sandy and Nicky had to say, Sheriff Green was also concerned.

SHERIFF: Listen, kids, I'll drive over to the mine and take a look around.

NICKY: Please, Sheriff, let us go with you.

SHERIFF: No, no, it's much too late. . . .

SANDY: But we can show you exactly where we found the plasmonium ore.

SHERIFF: Hmmm . . . well, I suppose that would be a help. All right; I'll come by and pick you up in a few minutes.

NARRATOR: Just a short time later, they were following the same route Dr. Royal and Dr. Parker had taken that afternoon.

NICKY: Look! There's Mom's car. So she *is* . . . what's that?

SOUND EFFECT: [*rumbling starts as Nicky speaks; gets louder and louder through the following speeches*]

SANDY: Oh, no!

SHERIFF: [*loudly*] This is zero-five-one calling Homebase. Zero-five-one calling Homebase. SOS! Do you read?

SOUND EFFECT: [*rumbling starts to get softer, then slowly fades away*]

NARRATOR: Within hours of the sheriff's call to headquarters, news of the trapped scientists had been picked up by Satellite News. Soon, reporters as well as rescue crews were on the spot.

NEWSCASTER: This is Bob Fredrickson for Satellite News reporting live from the Centripetal Corporation mine where Dr. Samantha Royal and Dr. Art Parker are trapped in a collapsed mine shaft. It is believed that last night's earth tremor caused the cave-in.

NARRATOR: Among those riveted to Satellite News were two people who had a very *personal* interest in what was going on—the owner and the manager of the Centripetal Corporation mine!

MINE MANAGER: How did Royal and Parker get in there, anyway?

MINE OWNER: I don't know. But we'd better hope they don't get out. Would you turn up the volume so I can hear this interview?

NEWSCASTER: [*slightly louder*] With me now is John Beebe, a member of the rescue team. John, how is the rescue operation progressing? Is it going as quickly as was hoped?

BEEBE: Well, Bob, the answer to that is yes and no. We're making good progress because the new laser-drivers we're using can cut through anything. What's slowing us down is the type of rock that has to be moved.

NEWSCASTER: What do you mean?

BEEBE: Well, some of the rocks we've encountered are unbelievably heavy. Even with our megalifters, we're limited in the number of rocks that can be moved at one time.

NEWSCASTER: What kind of rocks are they?

BEEBE: I really wouldn't know, Bob. But they're very unusual. They glow pink. Kind of pretty, actually.

NEWSCASTER: I understand that the . . .

SOUND EFFECT: [*hum of excited voices*]

NEWSCASTER: Uh-oh, something seems to be happening here. The sun is setting—and it's only eight o'clock in the morning! Excuse me, sir. Sir?

DR. GRAYBAR: Yes?

NEWSCASTER: Aren't you Dr. Graybar of World Science Laboratories?

DR. GRAYBAR: Yes, I am.

NEWSCASTER: Can you explain why the sun is going down at this hour of the day?

DR. GRAYBAR: I would say that the earth has suddenly tipped again. This is very serious. I'm sure there will be severe consequences. And I might add that Dr. Royal and Dr. Parker predicted this.

NEWSCASTER: Thank you, Dr. Graybar and Mr. Beebe. Now, back to our studio.

NARRATOR: A few minutes later, the head of the rescue operation came running out of the mine shaft with the news that the tipping of the earth had created a deep crevice that allowed rescuers to reach the trapped scientists.

MINE MANAGER: Boss! There's another news bulletin coming on. Quick! Something must have happened at the mine.

BEEBE: We've got 'em!

NEWSCASTER: Can you see Dr. Parker and Dr. Royal?

BEEBE: Yes! Yes! They're bringing them out!

SOUND EFFECT: [*cheering*]

SANDY/NICKY: Mom! Mom!

NEWSCASTER: Excuse me, Dr. Royal, Dr. Parker, do you have a few words for our Satellite News viewers?

DR. ROYAL: Sandy! Nicky!

SANDY: Mom! Are you all right?

NEWSCASTER: Ummm . . . excuse me . . .

NICKY: Are you okay, Mom? How about you, Dr. Parker?

DR. ROYAL: Well, we're a little bruised and very hungry, but otherwise I think we're okay.

DR. PARKER: And from what the sheriff told us, it's thanks to you two that we're here at all!

NEWSCASTER: Dr. Royal, Dr. Parker, you're glowing pink!

DR. ROYAL: That's because we're covered with plasmonium dust. Centripetal Corporation has secretly been mining plasmonium from the earth's core.

MINE MANAGER: Boss! Boss! Did you hear that?

MINE OWNER: Don't worry, Foster. They can't prove a thing. All the evidence has been buried in the cave-in!

NEWSCASTER: That's a strong accusation, Dr. Royal. Do you have any proof?

DR. ROYAL: See this camera? It tells the whole story.

MINE OWNER: I'm afraid that does it for us, Foster.

NARRATOR: In the days that followed, there was still a great deal to be done.

SOUND EFFECT: [*hum of many voices; banging of a gavel*]

DR. GRAYBAR: I've called this meeting because our problems are not over. The earth *must* be returned to its normal position. And it must be done *now,* before there is another earth tremor.

DR. ORTIZ: To accomplish that, plasmonium must be replaced in the earth's core. But how?

DR. KILE: Dr. Royal and Dr. Parker have been working on the production of artificial plasmonium. Perhaps we should ask them if they have any ideas.

DR. ROYAL: You're correct, Dr. Kile. We have managed to create a synthetic plasmonium in our laboratory by fusing hepalite and tungasium. We think it's a viable technique, but our research has not been tested in the field.

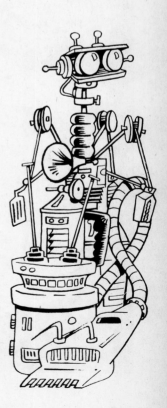

DR. GRAYBAR: You will have that opportunity now. It's our only hope.

NARRATOR: The crevice in the Centripetal mine that had been created by the last earth tremor was found to extend well beyond the earth's mantle. Did it go as far as the core? No one knew for sure, but they would soon find out.

NEWSCASTER: [*very quietly*] This is Bob Fredrickson of Satellite News on location in the mountains that surround the Centripetal Corporation mine. From where I'm standing, I can see the mine directly below me. I'm told that the mine crevice has been filled with hepalite and tungasium. Scientists are now ready to detonate a thermofusion explosion that they hope will result in the formation of plasmonium. This synthetic plasmonium will, in turn, be forced into the earth's core. The whole world is watching and waiting during this countdown to zero!

DR. PARKER: T minus thirty seconds and counting.

NEWSCASTER: Thirty seconds to the most important moment in the life of this planet.

DR. ROYAL: T minus ten seconds and counting. Nine . . . eight . . . seven . . . six . . . five . . . four . . . three . . . two . . . one . . . zero . . .

SOUND EFFECT: [*very loud explosion that continues for a few seconds; then more softly as the narrator speaks*]

NARRATOR: There was a tremendous roar. The earth shook as never before. After several minutes, there was silence. When the dust and debris settled, a huge crater could be seen where the Centripetal Corporation mine had once been. It was several minutes before anyone dared speak.

DR. GRAYBAR: What is the position of the sun?

DR. PARKER: Thirty-eight millibars northeast.

DR. ORTIZ: Exactly where it should be!

DR. ROYAL: It worked!

SOUND EFFECT: [*cheering and congratulations*]

NEWSCASTER: This is Bob Fredrickson for Satellite News. It's 8 A.M., the day after Countdown to Zero, as it's now being called. And now a report from the science desk. The first swarms of monarch butterflies were seen in Mexico yesterday, where scientists expected them to resume their normal migration patterns. The sun rose only once this morning, and I know I speak for all of us when I say that we certainly are glad!

Macmillan/McGraw-Hill

DR. ROYAL: Sandy! Nicky! Better turn off the TV and get ready to leave for school!

SANDY/NICKY: Okay, Mom!

SOUND EFFECT: [*TV being switched off*]

BLOCKING DIAGRAM

Arrange eleven chairs, as shown. The narrator and the newscaster can use music stands to hold their scripts.

1. NARRATOR
2. SANDY ROYAL
3. NICKY ROYAL
4. DR. SAMANTHA ROYAL
5. DR. ART PARKER

6. DR. KILE
7. DR. GRAYBAR
8. NEWSCASTER
9. SHERIFF GREEN

10. MINE OWNER
11. MINE MANAGER
12. JOHN BEEBE
13. DR. ORTIZ

SOUND EFFECTS

Your Readers Theater production of *Countdown to Zero* can be made even more effective and realistic with the addition of the sound effects specified in the script. Sound effects can be made by using the actual sound or by using something else that gives the illusion of the sound. Do some experimenting to invent your own methods for creating various sounds. Then test your sounds by recording them and listening to the playback. Here are a few things to consider when you are planning and executing sound effects:

- Will the sound effect appear realistic to a listening audience?
- Is the sound effect done at an appropriate volume?
- Does the sound effect last the proper length of time?

When you're satisfied with the sound you've produced, record it on a master tape. Be sure the sound effects are recorded in exactly the same order as they appear in the script. If the same sound effect is called for more than once, record it separately each time. Remember to allow time to start and stop the tape by letting the recorder run silently for about five seconds between effects.

When your Readers Theater group begins to rehearse the play, use the tape-recorded sound effects so you'll know how to gauge the "wait time" needed for the sound before saying the next line.

Macmillan/McGraw-Hill

CREATING SOUND EFFECTS

TV being switched on and off Record the click of a light switch, or a TV with the volume turned down. Or make a clicking sound with the tongue against the roof of the mouth.

scratching on wood Scratch on a wooden desk, table, or door.

door opening and closing Experiment with several doors and record the one that sounds the best.

knock at door Knock on a wooden door.

car starting; car stopping; car doors opening and closing You'll need the help of an adult to record a car engine starting. The sound of the motor being turned off followed by the opening and closing of the doors will signal that the car has stopped.

clinking and clanking of lab equipment Place silverware or other metal items in a box and rummage through them.

footsteps Record actual footsteps (the microphone should follow the walkers). The walkers should wear shoes, not sneakers, and walk on a bare floor. Decide in advance the pace at which each person should walk. To make the sound of receding footsteps, the microphone should remain in place instead of following the walker.

gasps; hum of excited voices Use your classmates. Rehearse them so that they sound natural; for example, they shouldn't gasp in unison!

banging of a gavel Sharply rap a wooden block on a desk or table.

dialing of telephone; phone being hung up Lift a telephone receiver. Depress the switch and dial. Then hang up.

phone ringing Tape the real thing for this sound.

footsteps walking or running over rocks and gravel Fill a bowl half full of a flake-type cereal and hold it close to the mike. Press two fingers in the flakes in a walking or running rhythm. For two people walking or running, double the bowls and the number of fingers.

running water Record the real thing, or pour water from a pitcher into another container that already has about an inch of water in it.

rumbling Put a handful of dried beans or macaroni in a small, deflated balloon. Then inflate the balloon and shake it. For a rumbling that gets louder and then fades away, begin with the volume of your tape recorder on *low*, increase it slowly to *loud*, then decrease slowly to *off*.

crash of something heavy falling Drop a heavy book or box on a desk.

muffled voice over the telephone Cup your hands together and place them over your nose and mouth. Speak naturally into your cupped hands.

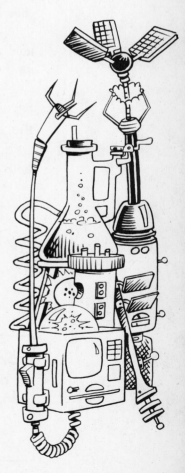

crackle of paper unfolding Prepare a sheet of notebook paper by folding it in half several times. As you record, unfold it close to the microphone.

computer Use the real thing, or record a hair dryer from a distance while typing on an electric typewriter.

crack of breaking wood Break several sticks.

creaking hinges Find a door that squeaks and record the sound while opening or closing it.

click of a light switch Use the real thing, or make a clicking sound with the tongue against the roof of the mouth.

whirring and hum of elevator Run a hair dryer at a distance. Keep it running as the readers speak. When the elevator is supposed to stop, turn off the hair dryer.

door sliding open Record a real elevator door opening. The sound made by a sliding cabinet or closet door could also be used.

static Crumple a piece of cellophane near the mike, or turn a radio dial to the far end and record the static noise.

bumping noises Hit an elbow against a door, or wrap a block of wood in a towel and knock it on a table.

papers rustling Rub two sheets of notebook paper together near the microphone.

cheering and congratulations Use your classmates. Ask them to say different things, such as *Yea* and *That's great*.

loud explosion Inflate a paper bag and pop it. At the same moment as the pop, create a rumbling sound. Let it fade slowly.

Select a studio director who can use hand signals to cue the sound-effects person and the readers. Both the studio director and the sound-effects person should have scripts with the sound effects highlighted.

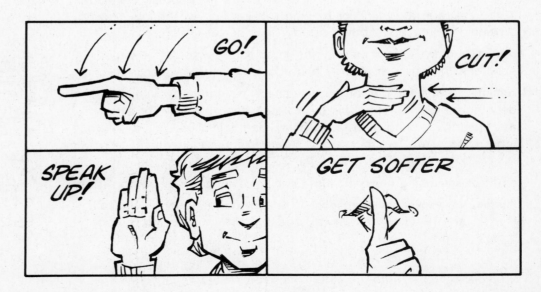

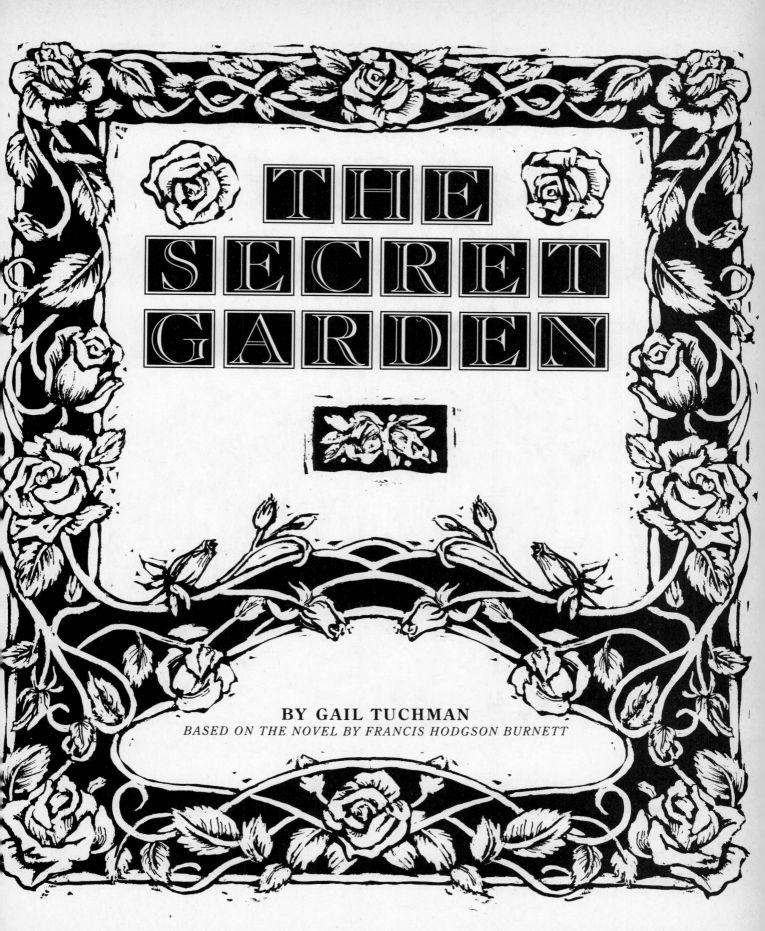

THE SECRET GARDEN

BY GAIL TUCHMAN
BASED ON THE NOVEL BY FRANCIS HODGSON BURNETT

Macmillan/McGraw-Hill

CAST

NARRATOR	MARTHA SOWERBY	ARCHIBALD CRAVEN
MRS. MEDLOCK	BEN WEATHERSTAFF	COLIN CRAVEN
MARY LENNOX	DICKON SOWERBY	DOCTOR

ACT I

NARRATOR: Mary Lennox was born in India in the 1890s. As a young child, she was cared for by an Indian servant, or ayah, who always gave Mary her own way in everything. As she grew up, inactivity left her pale and languid, and her ayah's catering made her as selfish as any tyrant who ever lived. Shortly after Mary's tenth birthday, an epidemic of cholera broke out in India, and people began dying like flies. It was in this strange and sudden way that Mary was left without parents or an ayah to care for her. And because she had no other relatives, she was sent to Yorkshire, England, to live with her uncle, Archibald Craven. Mrs. Medlock, her uncle's housekeeper, met Mary in London, and together they traveled to Mr. Craven's ancestral home, Misselthwaite Manor.

[Display transparency of Misselthwaite Manor (page 151).]

MRS. MEDLOCK: I may as well tell you something about where you are going. The house is six hundred years old, and it's on the edge of the moor. There's near a hundred rooms in it, though most of them's locked up tight. There's pictures and fine old furniture and a big park round it with gardens and trees—but there's nothing else. Well, what do you think of it?

MARY: Nothing. I know nothing about such places.

MRS. MEDLOCK: Don't you care?

MARY: It doesn't matter whether I care or not.

MRS. MEDLOCK: You're right. It doesn't. Your uncle is not going to trouble himself about you. That's sure and certain. He never troubles himself about no one. He's got a crooked back which set him wrong. He was a sour young man, and he got no good of all his money and big place till he married. His bride was a sweet, pretty thing. He'd have walked the world over to get her a blade o' grass she wanted. When she passed away . . .

MARY: Oh! Did she die?

MRS. MEDLOCK: Yes, and it made him stranger than ever. He won't see people, and most of the time he goes away. When he's home, he shuts himself up in the West Wing. You needn't expect to see him, and you mustn't expect there will be people to talk to. You'll have to play about and look after yourself. You'll be told what rooms you can go into and what rooms to keep out of. There's gardens enough, but when you're in the house, don't go poking about.

MARY: I shall not want to go poking about!

NARRATOR: When they arrived at the manor, Mary was led upstairs.

[*Display transparency of Mary's room* (page 152).]

MRS. MEDLOCK: Well, here you are! This room and the next one are where you'll be. You must keep to them. Don't you forget that!

NARRATOR: The next morning when Mary opened her eyes, she saw a young housemaid kneeling at the grate kindling a fire. Outside her window, Mary could see a great stretch of treeless land.

MARY: What is that? It looks like an endless, dull, purplish sea.

MARTHA: That's the moor. Does tha' like it?

MARY: No. I hate it!

MARTHA: That's because tha'rt not used to it. In time tha' will like it. I just love it. It's not bare. It's covered wi' growin' things as smells sweet. It's fair lovely in spring an' summer when the gorse an' broom an' heather's in flower. Mother raised twelve o' us in a cottage on the moor, an' the young ones still tumble about an' play out there all day. I wouldn't live away from the moor for anythin'.

MARY: In India, my ayah never spoke with me in this way. Are you to be my servant?

MARTHA: I'm to do the housemaid's work up here an' wait on you a bit, but you won't need much waitin' on.

MARY: Who will dress me?

MARTHA: Canna' tha' dress thysen!

MARY: What do you mean? I don't understand your language.

MARTHA: That's Yorkshire tha'rt hearin'. I mean, can't you put on your own clothes?

MARY: No, I never did in my life. My ayah always dressed me.

MARTHA: Well, it's time tha' should learn. It'll do thee good to wait on thysen a bit. My mother always said she couldn't see why grand people's children didn't turn out fools—what with bein' washed an' dressed an' took out to walk as if they was puppies!

NARRATOR: Mary suddenly felt so horribly lonely and far away from everything she understood that she began sobbing. But something friendly in Martha's Yorkshire speech had a good effect on her, and after a bit she stopped crying.

MARTHA: It's time for thee to wrap up warm an' run out an' play.

MARY: Who will go with me?

MARTHA: You'll go by yourself. My twelve-year-old brother, Dickon, goes off on the moor by himself and plays for hours. He's got a pony an' sheep on the moor that knows him, an' birds come an' eat out of his hand. However little there is to eat, he always saves a bit o' his bread to coax his pets.

MARY: Your Dickon sounds interesting. I should like to meet him.

MARTHA: Tha' might. Now, here's your coat an' hat. If tha' goes round that way, tha'll come to the gardens. There's lots o' flowers in summertime, but there's nothin' bloomin' now. One of the gardens is locked up, and no one has been in it for ten years. Your uncle had it shut when his wife died so sudden. It was her garden, an' he locked the door an' dug a hole an' buried the key.

MARY: A garden no one has been in for ten years! I wonder what it looks like. Can any flowers still be alive? How could a garden be shut up? How curious indeed. . . .

NARRATOR: Mary buttoned her coat and went outside. She spent many hours wandering through different gardens with ivy-covered walls. Suddenly, she stopped and looked more closely at one of the high stone walls.

[*Display transparency of the ivy-covered wall* (page 153).]

MARY: Martha mentioned a locked-up garden. I wonder if this could be the one. This wall looks as if it encloses a place on the other side. I can see the treetops above the wall and a beautiful bird on one of the branches! Perhaps he lives in the mysterious garden and knows all about it. I wonder why my uncle buried the key. If he liked his wife so much, why did he hate her garden?

NARRATOR: As Mary walked back toward the manor, she saw an old gardener. He took no notice of her, and so at last, she spoke to him.

MARY: There's no door into the garden on the other side of that wall. There are trees there, and a bird with a red breast is sitting on one of them and singing.

BEN: That's the robin. He comes when I whistle to him.

MARY: He's so pretty and cheerful. Does he always come when you call him?

BEN: Aye, that he does. I've knowed him ever since he was a fledgling when he come out of the nest in the garden. He was too weak to fly back over the wall for a few days an' we got friendly. When he went over the wall again, the rest of his brood was gone. He was lonely, an' he come back to me.

MARY: I'm lonely, too.

BEN: I'm Ben Weatherstaff, an' I'm lonely mysel' except when the robin is with me. He's the only friend I've got.

MARY: I have no friends at all. I've never had anyone to play with.

BEN: Tha' an' me are a good bit alike. We was both wove out of the same cloth. We're neither of us good-lookin' an' we're both of us as sour as we look. We've got the same nasty tempers, both of us, I'll warrant.

NARRATOR: Mary turned away from Ben and spoke to the robin.

MARY: Would you make friends with me, robin? Would you?

BEN: Why, tha' talked to the robin almost like Dickon talks to his wild things on the moor. The robin lives in the garden over the wall among the old rose trees.

MARY: Rose trees? I should like to see them. Where is the door? There must be a door somewhere.

BEN: There was a door ten year' ago, but there's no door anyone can find now. Don't you poke your nose where it's no cause to go. Get you gone to play, for I've no more time.

NARRATOR: Each day Mary grew more curious about the locked garden. As she walked and ran in the wind, the fresh air blown over the moor filled her lungs. It whipped red color into her cheeks, brightened her eyes, and gave her an appetite she'd never known before. One night during a storm, she was sitting with Martha.

[*Display transparency of Mary's room (page 152).*]

MARY: Why does Mr. Craven hate the garden?

MARTHA: Mrs. Medlock said it's not to be talked about. There's lots o' things in this place that's not to be talked over—by Mr. Craven's orders. But for the garden, he wouldn't be like he is. It was Mrs. Craven's garden that she had made when first they were married. They used to tend the flowers themselves, an' him an' her used stay there hours an' hours, readin' an' talkin'.

MARY: What happened to her? Mrs. Medlock said she died.

MARTHA: There was an old tree with a branch bent like a seat on it, an' she made roses grow over it, an' she used to sit there. But one day when she was sittin', the branch broke an' she fell on the ground an' was hurt so bad that next day she died. The doctors thought Mr. Craven would die o' sadness. That's why he hates the garden. No one's never gone in since, an' he won't let anyone talk about it.

MARY: I feel sorry for him. Wait . . . listen! What was that? Did you hear someone crying? It sounded like it came from one of the corridors.

MARTHA: No, no. It's the wind. Sometimes it sounds as if someone was lost on the moor an' wailin'. Or it's Betty Butterworth, the scullery maid who's had the toothache all day.

NARRATOR: The next night, Mary heard the crying sound again.

MARY: There *is* someone crying! There *is!*

[*Display transparency of the ivy-covered wall* (page 153).]

NARRATOR: A few days later, Mary went outside with a skipping rope that Martha's mother had sent her. Spring was coming and the earth was rich and ready for things to grow. Mary skipped alongside the ivy-covered wall near the locked-up garden and looked at the treetops. The robin chirped and hopped about to greet her.

MARY: You do remember me! Just look how close you let me come! You are prettier than anything else in the world.

NARRATOR: Mary watched the robin hop over to a small pile of freshly turned-up earth to look for a worm.

MARY: What a deep hole! Maybe a dog was digging here. Why, there's something sticking out of the soil. A . . . key! Perhaps it's the key to the garden! If I could find the door, I could open it and see what's inside the walls and what happened to the old rose trees. I must find that hidden door!

NARRATOR: The next day Mary went again to the walk beside the walled-in garden. The robin was there, swaying on a long branch of ivy. He greeted her with a chirp.

MARY: Hello, friend robin. Since you showed me where the key was yesterday, perhaps you will show me the door today.

NARRATOR: The robin flew to the top of the wall and sang. Suddenly a gust of wind waved the branches of the trees and swayed the ivy hanging from the wall. As the ivy trails swung to and fro, Mary spotted the tarnished knob of a door hidden under the leaves. With trembling hands, she drew the key from her pocket and inserted it into the keyhole.

MARY: The key fits! It fits!

NARRATOR: Mary took a long breath as she held back the curtain of ivy and slowly pushed the door open. Then she slipped through it and shut it tight behind her. She looked about, breathing fast with excitement, wonder, and delight. Mary was standing *inside* the secret garden.

[*Display transparency of the barren garden* (page 154).]

MARY: How still it is! How still! No wonder it's still. I am the first person who has spoken in here for ten years. It's the sweetest, most mysterious-looking place I've ever seen. I wonder if anything is alive. I don't see even a tiny bud anywhere, but I'm *inside* the wonderful garden, and I can come through the door under the ivy anytime. I've found a secret place all my own!

NARRATOR: Suddenly Mary saw some little pale-green points poking up out of the black earth.

MARY: It isn't a completely dead garden! There are living things here. I'll dig and weed until everything can breathe. I shall come every day to my secret garden and make it live again.

ACT II

[*Display transparency of Mary's room* (page 152).]

NARRATOR: That night Mary was so excited that she could hardly wait to talk with Martha.

MARY: Martha, does Dickon know about plants?

MARTHA: Why, Dickon can make a flower grow out of a brick wall. Mother says he just whispers things out o' the ground.

MARY: I wish . . . I wish I had a little spade. This is such a big, lonely place. If I had a spade, I might make a little garden.

MARTHA: Aye. And why not? Mother said diggin' an' rakin' would make tha' happy. I'll ask Dickon to bring thee some garden tools an' seeds.

MARY: Oh, thank you, Martha!

[*Display transparency of the ivy-covered wall* (page 153).]

NARRATOR: A few days later, Mary saw a boy sitting under a tree near the greenhouse. He was playing a wooden pipe, while squirrels, pheasants, and rabbits drew near to listen. When he saw Mary, he spoke to her in a low piping voice.

DICKON: Don't tha' move. It'll flight 'em. I'm Dickon, and I know tha'rt Miss Mary. I'll get up slow because if tha' makes a quick move, it startles 'em. A body 'as to move gentle an' speak low when wild things is about.

MARY: Did you get the garden tools and seeds?

DICKON: Aye. Sit thee on the log an' I'll tell thee what all the seeds will look like when they flower—an' how to plant 'em an' watch 'em an' feed an' water 'em. Where is tha' garden?

MARY: Can you keep a secret? It's a great secret, and I don't know what I should do if anyone found it out. I believe I should die!

DICKON: I'm keepin' secrets all the time. If I couldn't keep secrets from the other lads—secrets about fox cubs an' birds' nests—there'd be naught safe on the moor. Aye, I can keep secrets.

MARY: I've found a garden. Actually, I've stolen it. It isn't mine. It isn't anybody's for that matter. Nobody wants it and nobody cares for it and nobody ever goes into it. Perhaps everything is dead in it already. I don't know, and I don't care! Nobody has any right to take it from me when I care about it and they don't.

DICKON: Eh-h-h! Where is it?

MARY: Come with me and I'll show you. The door is hidden over here under the ivy. Here it is. Just a moment, and I'll have it unlocked.

NARRATOR: Mary turned the key and the two children walked through the little wooden door.

[*Display transparency of the barren garden* (page 154).]

DICKON: Eh! It is a strange, pretty place! It's as if a body was in a dream.

MARY: Will you help me make it come alive?

DICKON: I'll come every day if tha' wants, rain or shine. It'll be the best fun I ever had in my life—shut in here an' wakenin' up a garden.

MARY: Dickon, you're as nice as Martha said. You make the fifth person I like. I never thought I should like five people.

DICKON: Only five folk tha' likes? Who is the other four?

MARY: Your mother and Martha and the robin and Ben Weatherstaff. Does tha' like me?

DICKON: Eh, that I does! I like thee wonderful an' so does the robin, I do believe.

NARRATOR: When Mary returned to the house that afternoon, Martha was waiting for her.

MARTHA: Your uncle wants to see you in his study. Mother met him on the moor this mornin'. She said somethin' as put him in the mind to see you before he goes away tomorrow.

NARRATOR: Mary's heart began to thump as she changed her dress, brushed her hair, and followed the waiting Mrs. Medlock down the corridor, in silence. This was to be her first meeting with her uncle since she arrived at the manor. She hardly knew how she would be received by this man she'd heard so much about.

[*Display transparency of Mr. Craven's study (page 155).*]

MRS. MEDLOCK: This is Miss Mary, sir. I'll come back for her when you ring.

MR. CRAVEN: Come in, Mary. Are you well, child? Do they take good care of you?

MARY: Yes, sir.

MR. CRAVEN: You are very thin.

MARY: I am getting fatter.

MR. CRAVEN: I forgot you. I intended to send you a governess.

MARY: Please—please don't make me have a governess, yet.

MR. CRAVEN: That's what Martha's mother said. She thought you ought to get stronger before you had a governess.

MARY: Martha's mother knows all about children. I want to play outdoors. It makes me feel strong when the wind blows over the moor. I skip and run and look to see if things are beginning to stick out of the earth. I don't do any harm.

MR. CRAVEN: Don't look so frightened. You could not do any harm, child. You may do what you like. I am your guardian, though I am a poor one. I can't give you time and attention because I'm ill, but I wish you to be happy. Martha's mother thought you needed fresh air and freedom and running about, so play as much as you like. Is there anything you want? Toys, books, dolls?

MARY: Might I—might I have a bit of earth?

MR. CRAVEN: Earth! What do you mean?

MARY: To plant seeds in—to make things grow—to see them come alive.

MR. CRAVEN: A bit of earth? You can have as much earth as you want. You remind me of someone else who loved the earth and things that grow. When you see a bit of earth you want, take it, child, and make it come alive.

MARY: May I take it from anywhere—if it's not wanted?

MR. CRAVEN: Anywhere. You must go now because I'm tired. I shall say good-by to you now for I'll be away all summer.

NARRATOR: That night Mary was awakened by heavy rain and wind—and a sound that she had heard before.

MARY: I hear crying again. And this time I'm going to find out where it's coming from.

NARRATOR: As Mary walked from corridor to corridor, the faint crying sound led her on until she reached a large, heavy door. Slowly she pushed the door open and saw a boy with a thin face, the color of ivory, lying in a huge bed. Tears ran down his face. Mary tiptoed silently across the big room.

[*Display transparency of Colin's room* (page 156).]

COLIN: Who are you? Are you a ghost?

MARY: No. Are you one?

COLIN: No. I am Colin Craven. Who are you?

MARY: I am Mary Lennox. Mr. Craven is my uncle.

COLIN: He is my father.

MARY: Your father! No one ever told me he had a son.

COLIN: Come here. You *are* real. Where did you come from?

MARY: From my own room. I heard crying. Why were you crying?

COLIN: Because I couldn't go to sleep and my head ached.

MARY: Did no one ever tell you I had come to live here?

COLIN: They daren't. I should have been afraid you'd see me, and I won't let people see me or talk about me.

MARY: Oh, what a strange house this is! Everything is a kind of secret. Rooms are locked up and gardens are locked up—and you! Have you been locked up?

COLIN: No. I am ill, and I have to stay in bed. It tires me to be moved out of this room. My father doesn't want to see me, although sometimes he comes when I'm sleeping. My mother died when I was born, and it makes him miserable to look at me.

MARY: He doesn't want to see the garden again, either.

COLIN: What garden?

MARY: Oh! Just—just a garden your mother used to like. Have you been here always?

COLIN: Nearly always. I was at the seashore once, but people stared at me. I used to wear an iron thing to keep my back straight, but a doctor came from London and said it was stupid. He told them to take it off and keep me out in the fresh air. I hate fresh air. . . . Wait! I just realized something—we are cousins! How old are you?

MARY: I am ten, and so are you.

COLIN: How do you know that?

MARY: When you were born, the garden door was locked and the key was buried, and it has stayed locked up for ten years.

COLIN: What garden door was locked? Who did it? Where was the key buried?

MARY: No one will talk about it. I think they have been told not to answer questions.

COLIN: I would make them tell me. If I were to live, this place would someday belong to me. They would have to tell me.

MARY: Do you think you won't live?

COLIN: I don't suppose I shall. Ever since I remember anything, I have heard people say I shan't. At first they thought I was too little to understand, and now they think I don't hear. But I do. I don't want to live, but I don't want to die, either. I think about it until I cry and cry. I want to see the garden, and I want the key dug up. The servants here must do as I say, so I will make them take me there!

MARY: Oh, don't—please don't do that! If you tell anyone, it will never be a secret again. If no one knows but us, it will become *our* secret garden. I promise I shall look every day for the key to the garden door.

COLIN: I like the idea of a secret garden. You must look for the key and then come chat with me every day.

NARRATOR: Mary visited Colin again the next day and told him about Dickon and the moor. As the two cousins were talking and laughing, Colin's doctor and Mrs. Medlock walked in.

DOCTOR: What is this? I'm afraid there has been too much excitement, and excitement is not good for you, my boy.

MRS. MEDLOCK: But he does look rather better, sir.

DOCTOR: You must not talk too much, Colin; you must not forget you are ill, and you must not forget you're very easily tired.

COLIN: I *want* to forget all that. Mary helps me forget.

DOCTOR: Very well, but you must remember to stay calm during these visits. Mary, Colin is in very delicate health. He must avoid any upsets or excitement.

MARY: All right, Doctor. I understand.

NARRATOR: For a week it rained, and Mary and Colin spent hours in his room reading splendid books and talking. On the first sunny day, Mary went to the garden and found Dickon. She immediately told him about Colin.

[*Display transparency of the awakening garden* (page 157).]

MARY: When I talk with Colin, I have to be very careful in what I say about the secret garden. I want to get to know him first. He's not like you, Dickon. I don't know yet, *for sure*, if he can be trusted with the secret.

DICKON: Don't thee worry! It'll all be right. See how these has pushed up, an' these an these? Here's a whole clump o' crocuses burst into purple an' orange an' gold.

NARRATOR: Mary and Dickon ran all around the garden. Leaf buds were swelling on rose branches that had seemed dead. The children put their noses close to the earth and sniffed its warm spring perfume. They dug and pulled and laughed and watched the robin building a nest.

MARY: When we first came here, everything seemed dull and gray. Now the gray wall is changing. It's as if a green mist were creeping over it.

DICKON: Aye, an' it'll be greener an' greener till the gray's all gone. Can tha' guess what I was thinkin'? I was thinkin' that if Colin was out here he wouldn't be thinkin' how sick he feels. He'd be watchin' for buds to break on the rosebushes. He'd likely be healthier. I was wonderin' if we could get him to come out here an' sit under the trees.

MARY: I've been thinking about that, too, just as I've wondered if he could keep a secret. Do you think we could bring him here without anyone seeing us? You could push his chair as if we were going for a stroll in the big gardens.

DICKON: Us'd be just two children watchin' a garden grow, an' he'd be another. Two lads an' a lass just lookin' at the spring-time. It'd be better than doctor's stuff.

NARRATOR: It was late afternoon when Mary returned to the house. Colin was furious because she hadn't visited him earlier.

[*Display transparency of Colin's room (page 156).*]

COLIN: Why did you go out instead of coming to talk to me? You are a selfish thing!

MARY: Well, so are you! You're the most selfish person I ever saw.

COLIN: I'm not as selfish as you because I'm ill. I'm sure there is a bump coming on my back, and I'm going to die.

MARY: You're not! You just say that to make people feel sorry for you. I don't believe it!

COLIN: Get out of the room!

MARY: I'm going, Colin, and I won't come back!

NARRATOR: But Mary did go back to Colin's room later that night when Mrs. Medlock came to fetch her.

MRS. MEDLOCK: Miss Mary, please come with me! Colin's worked himself into hysterics, and he'll do himself harm. No one can do anything with him. You come and try. He likes you.

NARRATOR: Mary put on her dressing gown and followed a worried Mrs. Medlock. She could hear Colin's tantrum all the way down the corridor.

MARY: Colin, stop this! I hate you! Everybody hates you! You'll scream yourself to death, and I wish you would. If you scream another scream, I'll scream too. And I can scream louder than you, and I'll frighten you!

COLIN: I can't stop! I felt a bump. I felt it. I shall have a crooked back like my father, and then I shall die.

MARY: You didn't feel a thing. Half that ails you is temper and hysterics. It was only a hysterical bump. There's nothing the matter with your horrid back. Turn over and let me look at it! There's not a single bump there. There's not a bump as big as a pin, and if you say there is again, I shall laugh!

COLIN: Do you think . . . I could . . . live to grow up?

MARY: You probably will, if you do as you are told and not give way to your temper. And you must get out in the fresh air.

COLIN: I'll go out with you, Mary, and Dickon can push my chair. Take my hand—as a kind of making up.

ACT III

NARRATOR: The garden had reached the time when it seemed as if more beauty was bursting out of the earth every day. Quite suddenly it came into Mary's mind that this was the right moment to tell Colin about finding the garden.

MARY: Colin, can I trust you? I trusted Dickon because the moor animals and birds trust him. Can I trust you—for sure—*for sure?*

COLIN: Yes—oh, yes!

MARY: Dickon will come to visit you tomorrow, but that's not all. The rest is better. I found a hidden door under the ivy on the wall. It opens into the secret garden!

COLIN: Oh! Mary! Shall I see it?

MARY: Of course you shall! I found the key and got in weeks ago, but I daren't tell you because I was afraid I couldn't trust you—*for sure!* But that's changed now. Since the doctor has given permission for you to go out with Dickon and me, we will take you to the garden tomorrow!

NARRATOR: That night, Colin was so excited he could hardly sleep. Soon after breakfast, he was helped into his wheelchair. Dickon pushed it slowly and steadily while Mary walked alongside. When they got to the garden door, Mary checked to make sure nobody was watching. Then quickly she opened the door, and Dickon pushed the chair through with one strong, steady, splendid push. Colin looked round and round as Dicken and Mary had done.

[Display transparency of the awakening garden (page 157).]

MARY: The garden's different from when I first saw it. Little green leaves are covering all the gray. The flowers are beginning to bloom, and the trees are showing pink.

DICKON: An' a pink glow o' color is creepin' all over thee, too, Colin—over tha' face an' neck an' hands an' all.

COLIN: The sun feels warm upon my face—like a hand with a lovely touch. I shall get well! I shall! And I shall live forever and ever and ever!

DICKON: I'll push tha' chair round the garden.

COLIN: I feel like I'm being taken around the country of a king and queen and showed all its mysterious riches. Why look, that's a very old tree over there, isn't it? There's not a single leaf on it. It looks quite dead.

DICKON: Aye. But roses has climbed all over it, an' they will hide every bit o' the dead wood when they're full o' leaves an' flowers. It won't look dead then. It'll be the prettiest of all.

COLIN: It looks as if a big branch had been broken off.

DICKON: It's been done many a year. Eh! Look at the robin!

NARRATOR: As Colin watched the robin, Mary whispered to Dickon.

MARY: It's lucky that the robin came by. I was afraid Colin might ask more about the old tree. We can never tell him how it broke!

COLIN: I'm going to see everything grow here. I'm going to grow here myself. Look! Who's that peering at us over the wall from the top of the ladder? Does he know who I am?

NARRATOR: Ben Weatherstaff stared and gazed and gulped a lump down his throat. He answered in a shaky voice.

BEN: Aye. That I do—wi' tha' mother's eyes starin' at me out o' tha' face. Tha'rt the poor bent lad.

COLIN: I'm not bent! I'm not!

NARRATOR: Colin's anger filled him with strength. He tore the coverings off his legs and shouted.

COLIN: Dickon, come here this minute! Hold my arms!

MARY: He can do it! He can!

COLIN: Just look at me!

DICKON: Why, he's standin' as straight as I am! He's as straight as any lad i' Yorkshire!

NARRATOR: Ben choked and gulped and suddenly tears ran down his wrinkled cheeks as he struck his hands together.

BEN: The lies folks tell! Tha'lt live to be a man yet. Bless thee!

COLIN: This is my garden. And you mustn't dare say a word about it! Come down from that ladder so I can talk to you. You will have to be in on our secret now.

NARRATOR: While Mary brought Ben Weatherstaff in through the hidden door, Colin tried to walk.

COLIN: I'm going to walk to that tree, and when I want to sit, I will sit, but not before. Everyone thought I was going to die. But I'm not.

BEN: Tha' die? Tha's got too much pluck in thee. Sit thee down on the ground a bit, young master.

COLIN: What work do you do in the gardens?

BEN: Anythin' I'm told to do. I'm kep' on by favor—because tha' mother liked me.

COLIN: My mother? This was her garden, wasn't it?

BEN: Aye, it was that, and she was very fond of it.

COLIN: It's my garden now, and I'm fond of it. I shall come here every day, but it's to be a secret. Dickon and Mary have made it come alive, and now you can come to help.

BEN: I've come here before when no one saw me. The last time was about two year' ago.

COLIN: But no one's been in it for ten years! There was no door!

BEN: I come over the wall, but the rheumatics held me back the last two year'. Mrs. Craven was so fond of the garden. She says to me, "Ben, if ever I'm ill or if I go away, you must take care of my roses." When she did go away, the orders was no one was ever to come here. But I come over the wall, and I did a bit o' work once a year. She gave her order first.

COLIN: I'm glad you did it. You'll know how to keep the secret.

BEN: Aye. I'll know. An' twill be easier for a man wi' rheumatics to come in at the door.

NARRATOR: On the grass near the tree, Mary had dropped her trowel. Colin stretched out his hand for it.

COLIN: Mary, let me have that trowel so I can dig in the earth.

BEN: I can get thee a rosebush to plant.

COLIN: Good! I want to do it before the sun goes down.

BEN: Here, lad. Mind the thorns. Set the plant in the earth thysel'.

NARRATOR: Colin's thin white hands shook as he set the rose in the hole that Dickon had helped him dig.

COLIN: It's planted! And the sun is only slipping over the edge. Help me up, Dickon. I want to be standing when it sets. That's part of the beauty.

NARRATOR: There *was* beauty in the garden, and it seemed to intensify in the months that followed. One day, Colin called Mary, Dickon, and Ben Weatherstaff together under the old tree.

[*Display transparency of the garden in bloom* (page 158).]

COLIN: Since I've been in the garden, I've had a strange feeling of being happy, as if something were pushing and drawing in my chest and making me breathe fast. Everything here makes me happy—the leaves and trees, the flowers and birds, the foxes and squirrels, and all of you. Beauty is all around us. The beauty in this garden has made me stand up and know I'm going to live to be a man. The beauty in this garden will push and draw me and make me grow strong so that I can walk and run like other children.

NARRATOR: Colin began to exercise, eat, laugh, and grow stronger, and Mary began to change, too. Her hair became thick and healthy-looking, and she had a bright color and lost her sour look. Like Colin and Mary, everything in the secret garden thrived and bloomed. The eggs in the robin's nest hatched, and the fledglings took their first flight.

COLIN: I wish my father would come home so I could show him the garden!

NARRATOR: While the secret garden was coming alive, Archibald Craven was wandering in faraway places. One day, he sat beside an icy mountain stream and looked at a mass of blue flowers—forget-me-nots.

MR. CRAVEN: It seems so long ago that I used to look at such flowers. They're so lovely. . . . I almost feel as if—as if I were coming alive again. Last night, I had a dream that my precious wife, Lilias, was calling me back to the garden. How strange it is that this morning I received a letter from Martha's mother suggesting I come home. Some secret force is drawing me home. I must go back to Misselthwaite at once! I've been filled with such terrible sorrow for ten years, but I want to do something now to set things right. I'll try to find the key to the garden and open the door. I must, though I don't know why.

[*Display transparency of the garden in bloom* (page 158).]

NARRATOR: Upon his arrival at the the manor, Mr. Craven went directly to the garden. Mary and Colin were having a race, and when Archibald Craven got to the garden door—at that precise moment—Colin burst through the door at full speed, almost into his father's arms!

MR. CRAVEN: Good heavens! Who . . . who are you?

COLIN: Father, I'm Colin. Can you believe it? I hardly can myself.

MR. CRAVEN: You're in the garden. In the garden!

COLIN: It was the garden that did it—and Mary and Dickon and Ben and the robin. I'm going to live forever, Father. Aren't you glad?

MR. CRAVEN: Take me into the garden, my boy, and tell me all about it.

NARRATOR: Mr. Craven held his son and Mary as they told him all about the secret garden. A little while later, Mrs. Murdock and Martha stood at the windows and gaped as they watched the master of Misselthwaite striding across the lawn. He had not looked this way in ten years. On one side of him skipped the young girl from India, flushed and happy. And on his other side, with his head up in the air and his eyes full of laughter, walked Master Colin—as strongly and steadily as any boy in Yorkshire!

locking iagram

Arrange eight chairs, as shown. The narrator can use a music stand to hold the script.

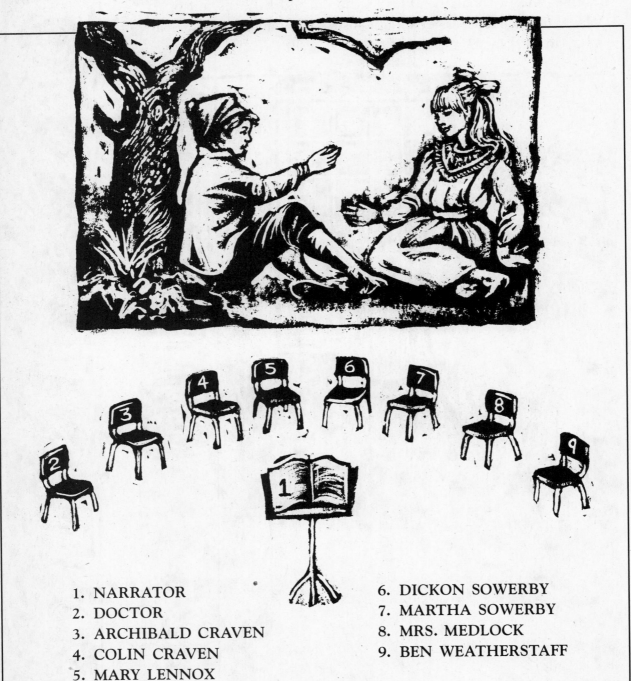

1. NARRATOR
2. DOCTOR
3. ARCHIBALD CRAVEN
4. COLIN CRAVEN
5. MARY LENNOX

6. DICKON SOWERBY
7. MARTHA SOWERBY
8. MRS. MEDLOCK
9. BEN WEATHERSTAFF

Macmillan/McGraw-Hill

ostume uggestions

Narrator This performer does not need a special costume, but a jacket and string tie for a boy reader or a long skirt for a girl could help the performer feel more in character.

Mrs. Medlock As housekeeper at Misselthwaite Manor, this character can wear a long dark skirt and blouse. A brooch or large pin could be used to fasten a velvet ribbon at the neck.

Mary Lennox Mary can wear a dark blouse and a mid-calf skirt or jumper. Dark tights and a large hair bow would also be appropriate.

Martha Sowerby As parlor maid, Martha can wear a blouse and a long skirt covered by a white apron. This character can pin a doily or lace hanky on her head to simulate a maid's cap.

Ben Weatherstaff A long-sleeved work shirt, wool vest, worn-looking pants with suspenders, cap, and boots would be fine for this character.

Dickon Sowerby Dickon can be dressed like Ben, with knickers instead of pants. Knickers can be made by tucking pant legs into knee socks and "blousing" the pants at the knee.

Archibald Craven and the Doctor
These readers should have a somber appearance; dark pants and jackets, white shirts, and black cravats are suggested.

Colin Craven For the scenes that take place inside the house, Colin can wear a long-sleeved white shirt or smock that resembles a nightshirt. The garment should be large enough to conceal his clothes. When the scene shifts to the garden, the performer can remove the shirt to reveal knickers, a sport coat, and bow tie.

 ackdrops

Backdrops for *The Secret Garden* can be created by reproducing the following transparency patterns on acetate and having students color them with markers. Position an overhead projector out of the sight lines of the audience. Following the cues in the script, project the transparencies onto a light-colored wall or screen behind the cast.

Macmillan/McGraw-Hill

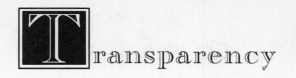 **T**ransparency **P**attern

Transparency Pattern

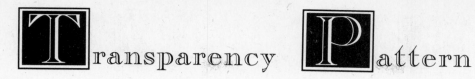Transparency Pattern

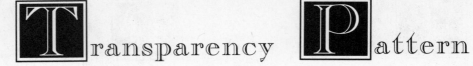

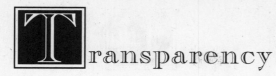 

Transparency Pattern

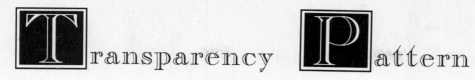 

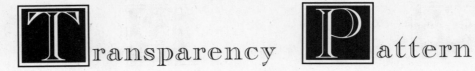

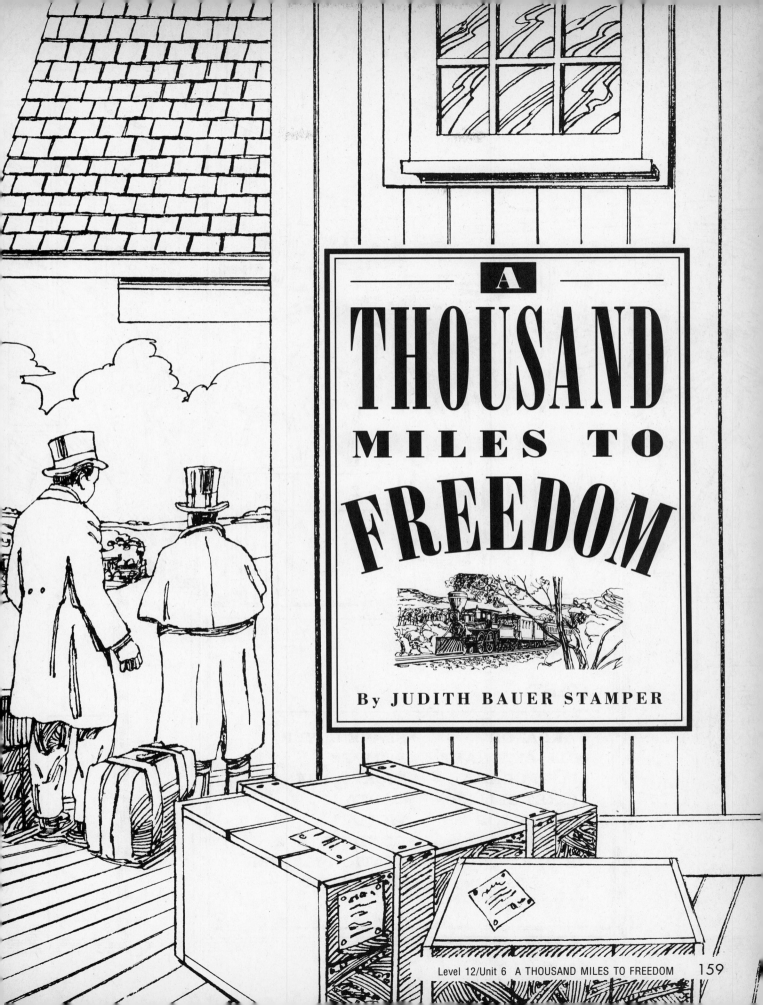

A THOUSAND MILES TO FREEDOM

By JUDITH BAUER STAMPER

CAST

NARRATOR

WILLIAM CRAFT

ELLEN CRAFT

TICKET SELLER

CONDUCTOR 1

MR. CRAY

DRIVER

PASSENGER

CAPTAIN 1

SLAVE BUYER

POMPEY

TICKET AGENT

CAPTAIN 2

WOMAN

CONDUCTOR 2

STATION MASTER

ONLOOKER

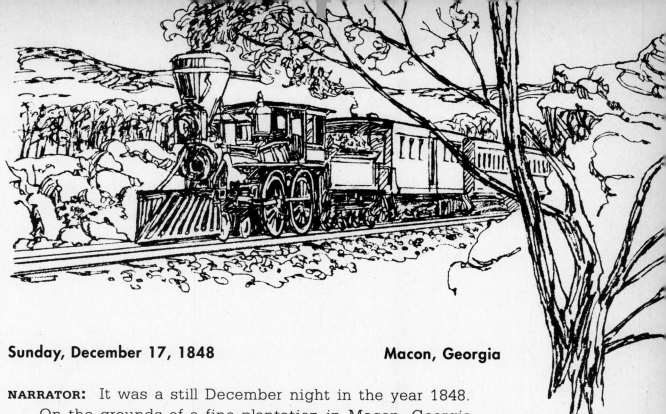

Sunday, December 17, 1848   **Macon, Georgia**

NARRATOR: It was a still December night in the year 1848. On the grounds of a fine plantation in Macon, Georgia, a light burned in a small cabin near the main house. Inside, a young couple talked. Ellen Craft gave every appearance of being white, with her fair skin and straight hair, so like her father. However, as the daughter of a black woman, she was obliged by law to follow her mother's condition. And so she was as much a slave as her mother—and as her husband, William Craft. As the couple spoke, their voices were hushed, not due to the lateness of the hour, but rather to the subject of their discussion.

WILLIAM: Ellen, listen! I got a plan, and I think it'll work!

ELLEN: A plan for our escape, William? What is it? Tell me!

WILLIAM: You'll pretend to be white, and I'll travel with you as your manservant.

ELLEN: But no white lady travels alone with a male slave.

WILLIAM: That's so. But you won't be a white *lady*. You'll dress yourself up as a young white gentleman—a sickly gentleman needing help. We'll take the train north, to Philadelphia and freedom!

ELLEN: Oh, William, we don't dare! Pretending to be white would be hard enough, but I could never act the part of a white gentleman for a journey of a thousand miles.

WILLIAM: Ellen, listen to me. Think of what'll happen if we don't dare. We'll belong to our masters forever—slaves to be bought and sold.

ELLEN: I think of nothing else! If we had children, they'd be the master's property, too. They could be torn away from us at any time. I could not bear it! . . . You're right, William. We must dare. Let us get the things we need for the disguise; with God's help, I will try to carry out the plan.

NARRATOR: William Craft was what was called a town slave. Trained in woodworking, his master hired him out to a cabinetmaker, a Mr. John Knight. William's wages went to his master, but he was allowed to keep the money that he made by working overtime. It was with these savings that the couple planned to finance their flight to freedom. Over the next few days, William went to different parts of town at odd times to purchase the articles they needed: a coat, a shirt, a hat, boots, and a pair of dark-green spectacles for Ellen. He couldn't find trousers small enough, so Ellen carefully stitched them herself. At last, the disguise was assembled.

Macmillan/McGraw-Hill

WILLIAM: We're ready. All that needs doing is to get visiting passes for a few days over Christmas. Most likely your mistress won't refuse—with you being her favorite slave and all.

ELLEN: I'll say I want to visit my dying old aunt for Christmas.

WILLIAM: And I'll ask Mr. Knight if I can go with you. He's a mighty suspicious man, but since I've never asked for a pass before, maybe he'll say yes. . . . If no one 'spects us back till after Christmas, they won't be looking for us till we're safe in Philadelphia. I surely pray we get those passes.

NARRATOR: The next day, William returned to the cabin with the precious paper in his pocket. He showed it to Ellen.

ELLEN: And here is mine!

WILLIAM: It's a wonder, Ellen. These papers are life or death to us, and we can't even read 'em.

ELLEN: Cannot read. . . . Oh, William, our plan will never work. I just remembered something I heard my mistress say. Travelers must write their names in a book when staying in a hotel, as well as at the Custom House in Charleston, South Carolina. And I can neither read *nor* write my name. We are lost, William, we are lost!

NARRATOR: Sitting in their little room that night, Ellen and William were on the verge of despair. All at once, Ellen raised her head, a smile replacing her tears.

ELLEN: William, it has come to me. You'll bandage my right hand and bind it up in a sling. Then it would seem right for me to ask someone at the hotel to write my name for me!

WILLIAM: Yes! That'll do it!

ELLEN: Perhaps, too, I should bind some herb poultices under my chin with strips of cloth. The bandages will add to my sickly appearance and hide the fact that I have no beard.

WILLIAM: We'll make you look like you're sufferin' from a mighty bad toothache!

NARRATOR: William and Ellen worked all through the night reviewing their plans and making their preparations. As a personal maid in the big house, Ellen had learned much. Though she could not read or write, she was as well-spoken as her mistress. As a house servant, she often overheard conversations about trips up North. She had stored in her mind information that might someday prove helpful to her and to William. Now that day had finally come.

Macmillan/McGraw-Hill

Thursday, December 21, 1848

**From Macon, Georgia
To Savannah, Georgia**

NARRATOR: Shortly before dawn, William cut Ellen's hair. Then he helped her on with the disguise.

WILLIAM: Hold still while I fasten this bow tie. You surely do make a most respectable gentleman. People'd never guess a slave is hiding behind those spectacles and bandages.

ELLEN: I hope you're right, William. I fear the next few days may be worse than the twenty-two years I've spent as a slave.

WILLIAM: It's time to blow the candle out now. Hold my hand, and let us pray for success. Think of it—freedom for Christmas!

NARRATOR: A few moments later, they rose and stood together in breathless silence. What if someone had been about the cabin listening and watching their movements? William took his wife by the hand, stepped to the door, drew it open, and peeped out. Though there were trees surrounding the cabin, the foliage scarcely moved. In fact, everything appeared to be as still as death.

WILLIAM: [*whispering*] Come, my dear. I will latch the door behind us one last time.

ELLEN: Now that the hour has finally come, I am so afraid.

WILLIAM: Me, too, Ellen. I've never been so scared. Every inch of this thousand miles seems like a mountain. But we've got to go on! There's no turning back now!

ELLEN: You are right, William. I'm ready now. We must have faith that God is on our side.

NARRATOR: They stepped out as softly as moonlight upon the water and tiptoed cautiously across the yard into the street. They scarcely breathed for fear of waking the sleeping household.

WILLIAM: This is where I leave you, Ellen, for we cannot be seen together in Macon. Do you remember what you must do?

ELLEN: Yes. From this moment, I must act as Mr. William Johnson, on my way to Philadelphia to seek medical advice. My slave, William, is along to attend me. I will go to the train station now and buy our tickets to Savannah, Georgia.

WILLIAM: And I'll board the last car with the other slaves. I'll look for you on the platform in Savannah.

NARRATOR: They walked separately, in different directions, to the railway station. Ellen felt both excitement and fear. Pretending to be free, she suddenly felt free—but real freedom was still a thousand miles away. As she walked into the red-brick station, she reminded herself of all the gestures a young, white gentleman might use—flicking lint from a coat lapel or hooking his thumbs in his vest pockets. Then she squared her shoulders and walked up to the ticket window.

ELLEN: Two tickets to Savannah, please. One for myself and one for my slave.

TICKET SELLER: Here you are, sir. Have a pleasant journey.

ELLEN: I thank you kindly, sir.

CONDUCTOR 1: A-l-l aboard!

NARRATOR: From his seat in the car at the end of the train, William watched Ellen board one of the front carriages. Then, in amazement and horror, he saw Mr. Knight, the cabinetmaker for whom he worked, rush across the train platform. He began looking suspiciously at the passengers in each of the carriages.

WILLIAM: It's Mr. Knight! Why would he be looking for me so soon?

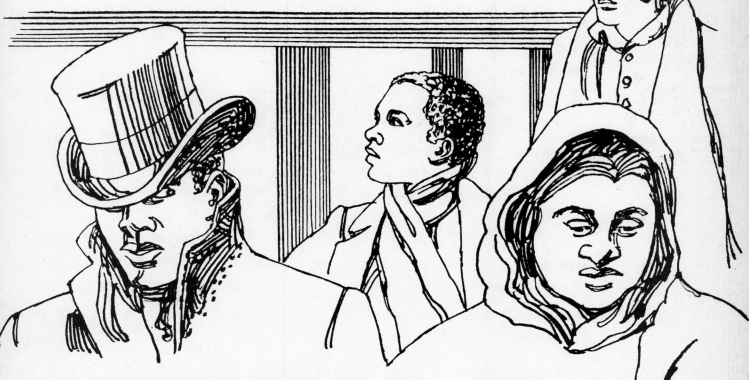

NARRATOR: Mr. Knight moved from one car to another, coming closer and closer to where William sat. With a pounding heart, William shrank into a corner and turned his face away from the door.

CONDUCTOR 1: A-l-l aboard!

NARRATOR: William expected to be grabbed from his seat at any moment. Suddenly, the train's whistle blew and the wheels began to turn. Mr. Knight jumped down from the train onto the platform as the train began to pick up speed. Only then did William sit up in his seat and begin to breathe more freely. But he might not have breathed quite so freely had he known that at this very moment, in another carriage, "Mr. Johnson" was also facing a fearful encounter.

MR. CRAY: It's a very fine morning, sir.

NARRATOR: It was Mr. Cray speaking. He was a friend of Ellen's master, and he had taken a seat next to "Mr. Johnson"! Fearful that Mr. Cray might recognize her voice, Ellen pretended not to hear.

MR. CRAY: [*in a louder voice*] It's a very fine morning, sir.

NARRATOR: Again, he did not receive an answer.

MR. CRAY: I will make him hear! [*loudly*] It's a very fine morning, sir!

ELLEN: Yes . . . yes, it is.

MR. CRAY: Poor fellow, he must be deaf. I shall not trouble him anymore.

NARRATOR: "Mr. Johnson" breathed a little easier, but was very glad when Mr. Cray got off the train several stops later. Finally, as evening fell, the train pulled into the Savannah station. "Mr. Johnson" stepped down off the train and saw William waiting on the platform.

WILLIAM: You must find a carriage, master. I'll follow behind with the bags.

ELLEN: Of course, William. There's a carriage at the station entrance. We'll take it.

DRIVER: Might you be going to the Charleston steamer, sir?

ELLEN: Yes, I am.

DRIVER: Right this way, then. Let me help you, sir. I can see that you are not well. Your slave can ride up on top.

ELLEN: I thank you, sir.

NARRATOR: The carriage took William and Ellen through the streets of Savannah to the steamer bound for Charleston, South Carolina. Soon after boarding, "Mr. Johnson" retired to his cabin to avoid encountering the other passengers. William followed behind with the bags. The minute the door shut behind them, Ellen pulled off her spectacles and hugged her husband.

Macmillan/McGraw-Hill

ELLEN: Oh, William, what a trial. When Mr. Cray sat down beside me, it was all I could do to keep myself from jumping off that train! But we did it, William. They believed me!

WILLIAM: I was sure we'd be caught when I saw old Mr. Knight come looking through the carriages. But as neither man recognized you, I do believe we've got a chance!

ELLEN: William, did you hear the others talking as we boarded? They think it odd that I retired so early. Perhaps you had better warm some flannel cloths and liniment by the stove where all are sure to notice you.

WILLIAM: The smell alone will make it mighty clear you're ill.

NARRATOR: The passengers certainly did take notice of William.

PASSENGER: What is that you've got there?

WILLIAM: Opodeldoc liniment, sir, for my master's rheumatism.

PASSENGER: It stinks enough to kill or cure twenty men! Away with it, or I reckon I'll throw it overboard!

NARRATOR: Satisfied that he had accomplished his purpose, William took the cloths and the opodeldoc back to his master's cabin. He waited a few minutes and then went back on deck, where he met the ship's captain.

WILLIAM: Begging your pardon, sir. Where do slaves sleep, sir?

CAPTAIN 1: Slaves? We have no sleeping accommodations set aside for your kind on this ship. You can sleep standing up for all I care!

NARRATOR: So William paced the deck for several hours, and then found some cotton sacks in a warm spot near the funnel. He dozed there, waiting for morning, when he would assist his master in preparing for breakfast.

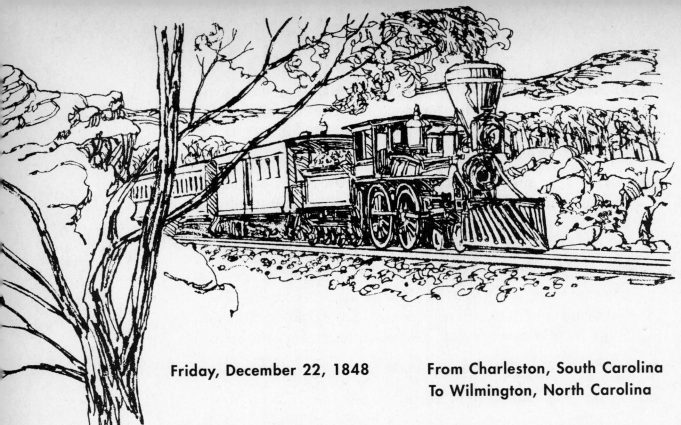

Friday, December 22, 1848   From Charleston, South Carolina
                                   To Wilmington, North Carolina

NARRATOR: At breakfast, "Mr. Johnson" was seated beside the captain in the ship's dining room.

CAPTAIN 1: Good morning, sir. How are you feeling today?

PASSENGER: I do hope your rheumatism is improved this morning?

ELLEN: Thank you both. I passed a comfortable night.

NARRATOR: Since "Mr. Johnson" had one arm in a sling, William cut his master's food and then went out.

CAPTAIN 1: You have a very attentive slave, sir, but you had better watch him like a hawk when you get North. He seems all very well here, but he may act quite differently there. I've known many a gentleman who have lost their slaves among them cutthroat abolitionists.

NARRATOR: Before "Mr. Johnson" could speak, a man sitting across the table joined the conversation.

SLAVE BUYER: Sound doctrine, Captain, very sound. I would not take a slave North under no consideration. If you do, he's as good as gone. He'll run away the first chance he gets. Now, stranger, if you've a mind to sell that slave, I'm your man. Just mention your price, and if it isn't out of the way, I will pay for him right here and now in hard silver dollars. What do you say, stranger?

ELLEN: I thank you for your offer, but I don't wish to sell, sir. I cannot get on well without him.

SLAVE BUYER: You will have to get on without him if you take him up North. I can tell you as a friend, he'll leave you the minute he crosses Mason and Dixon's line.

ELLEN: I think not, sir. I have great confidence in William's fidelity.

SLAVE BUYER: Fidelity! Fidevil! You use a word like "fidelity" for a slave! It always makes me mad to hear a man talking about fidelity in slaves. There ain't a one of 'em who wouldn't take off if he had half a chance!

CAPTAIN 1: Excuse me, gentlemen, we are approaching Charleston. I am sure you all will want to go out on deck.

ELLEN: Thank you, Captain, but I fear the sea air is too much for my constitution to bear. If you'll excuse me, sir, I'd best retire to my cabin.

NARRATOR: Ellen walked slowly back to the cabin, shaking with anger. William was waiting by the door for her return.

WILLIAM: I could hear that slave buyer a-shouting clear out on deck. What'd he say?

ELLEN: He offered to buy you, William! Thank goodness we're pulling into port. It looks as if we've made it to Charleston, South Carolina.

WILLIAM: Just look at that crowd on the wharf. That could mean trouble for us. It's possible someone in that crowd might recognize me. We'd better wait until things clear out 'fore leaving the ship.

ELLEN: I pray our absence hasn't been discovered. If it has been, they may have telegraphed for someone to stop us on shore.

NARRATOR: William and Ellen waited until all the other passengers had gone ashore. When they saw that no one lingered on the wharf, they took a carriage from the steamer to a hotel that Ellen had heard about. While "Mr. Johnson" rested, William took his master's boots out on the back steps to polish them. While he was sitting there, one of the hotel slaves engaged him in conversation.

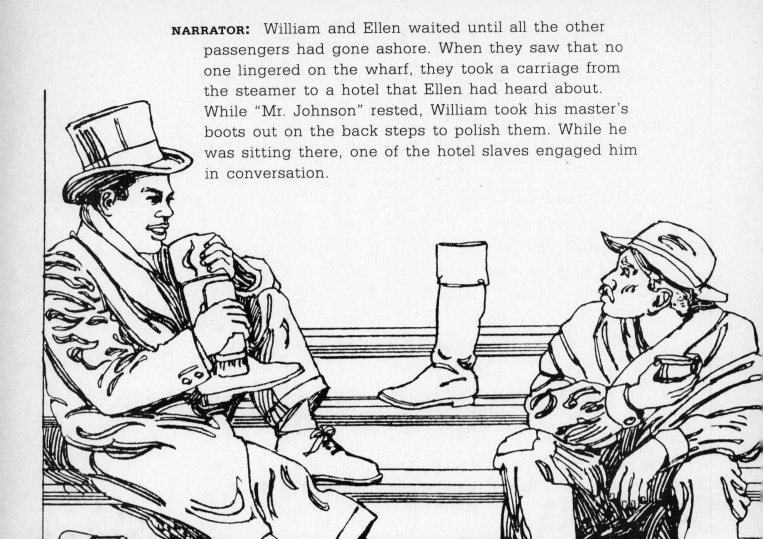

POMPEY: Where you headed, brother?

WILLIAM: Philadelphia.

POMPEY: Philadelphia! I hear there're no slaves in Philadelphia.

WILLIAM: I heard the same.

POMPEY: I surely do wish I was going with you! How you getting there?

WILLIAM: We're taking the steamer from Charleston to Philadelphia.

POMPEY: That's what you think—that steamer don't run in the winter, brother. You know, a few weeks back, they found a runaway slave hiding on board. They whipped him good and sent him back to his master.

WILLIAM: Poor soul! Well, I guess my master will know another way to Philadelphia.

POMPEY: I hope when you get there, you stay!

WILLIAM: Thank you, brother. I best be going now.

NARRATOR: When William returned to the room with the well-shined boots, he told Ellen what he had learned.

WILLIAM: We gotta change our plans, Ellen. It may be just as well for us. Since that runaway slave was found, I got a suspicion they're going to check all the slaves mighty carefully.

ELLEN: I heard a passenger describing another way—the Overland Mail Route. We'd have to take a steamer to Wilmington, North Carolina, and a train from there to Philadelphia.

WILLIAM: We're all right then! We should leave right after dinner.

NARRATOR: Upon leaving the hotel, William and Ellen took a carriage to the Charleston Custom House office. There "Mr. Johnson" would buy the tickets through to their final destination, Philadelphia—but not without obstacles.

ELLEN: Two tickets to Philadelphia, please. One for me and one for my slave.

TICKET AGENT: Just a minute, sir. . . . Hey you, come over here!

WILLIAM: You talking to me, sir?

TICKET AGENT: Of course I'm talking to you! Do you belong to this gentleman?

WILLIAM: Yes, sir, I do.

TICKET AGENT: That's all right then. Now, sir, I wish you to register your name here and also the name of your slave. You'll also have to pay a dollar duty on him.

ELLEN: Here is the dollar, sir. But, as you can see, I cannot write because of my bandaged arm. Would you kindly register the names for me?

TICKET AGENT: Regulations forbid me from doing that, sir! Either you register the names yourself or you'll not pass through my station.

NARRATOR: The man spoke so harshly that he attracted the attention of other passengers in the Custom House. It was a tense moment. Ellen found herself scarcely breathing. Just then, a passenger who had sat at breakfast with "Mr. Johnson" stepped forward. He patted "Mr. Johnson" on the shoulder and then turned to the ticket agent.

PASSENGER: See here, sir! Mr. Johnson is well known to me, and I will vouch for him. Anyone can see that he is unwell. There is no reason to treat him so unkindly.

TICKET AGENT: I am simply following the rules, sir.

CAPTAIN 2: What is all this commotion about? I'm the captain of the steamer bound for Wilmington. We're about to leave, and these passengers must board. I will register the gentleman's name and assume the responsibility upon myself. Your full name, sir?

ELLEN: William Johnson.

CAPTAIN 2: William Johnson and slave. There, it's done. Everything is in order now, Mr. Johnson.

ELLEN: Thank you, Captain. You have my deepest gratitude, sir.

CAPTAIN 2: I'm sure the ticket agent intended no disrespect, Mr. Johnson. They have to be very vigilant in Charleston; otherwise, those blamed abolitionists might make off with any number of slaves.

ELLEN: I am sure you are right, Captain. I am sure you are right.

NARRATOR: "Mr. Johnson" trembled at their narrow escape. How close they had come to being sent back! He could only imagine what other troubles might lie ahead.

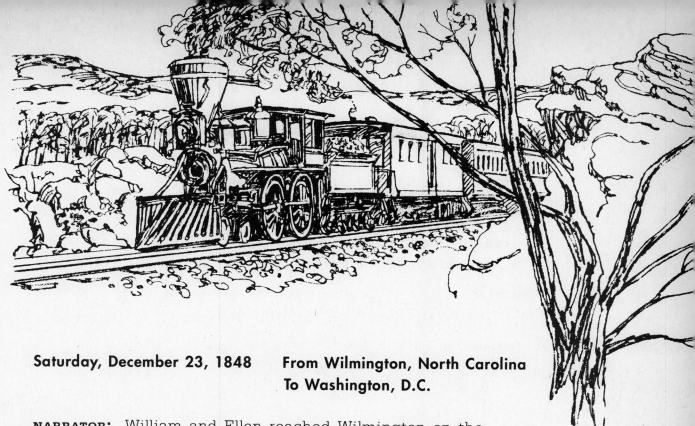

**Saturday, December 23, 1848   From Wilmington, North Carolina
To Washington, D.C.**

NARRATOR: William and Ellen reached Wilmington on the third morning of their journey. There they boarded a train that took them to Richmond and then on to Fredericksburg, Virginia. Outside Fredericksburg, they boarded a steamer bound for Washington, D.C. During the trip, "Mr. Johnson" met many white people whose kindness posed great danger. One man presented him with his business card. "Mr. Johnson" quickly put it in a pocket for he couldn't risk holding it upside down while pretending to read it! Two young ladies offered their shawls to make a pillow for the ailing gentleman. Evidently, the disguise was convincing. However, "Mr. Johnson" could never let down his guard. There was no way to know when danger might strike—or in what form.

WOMAN: Oh, my goodness, there goes my slave Ned. That's him, over there!

ELLEN: Madam, I fear you are mistaken. That's my slave William!

NARRATOR: The woman paid no attention to "Mr. Johnson's" protests.

WOMAN: You, Ned, come here to me, you runaway!

ELLEN: I assure you, madam, that you are mistaken!

NARRATOR: "Mr. Johnson's" blood ran cold. What would he do if the woman continued to insist that William was her Ned? Would he be asked to produce ownership papers?

WOMAN: Come closer, Ned. I know it's you, you rascal!

WILLIAM: Excuse me, missus. I'm William.

NARRATOR: The woman looked closely at William and then turned to "Mr. Johnson."

WOMAN: Oh, I do beg your pardon, sir. I was so sure he was my Ned! But indeed you were right. I was mistaken.

NARRATOR: "Mr. Johnson" breathed a sigh of relief. Their luck had held once again. If only it would last a little longer.

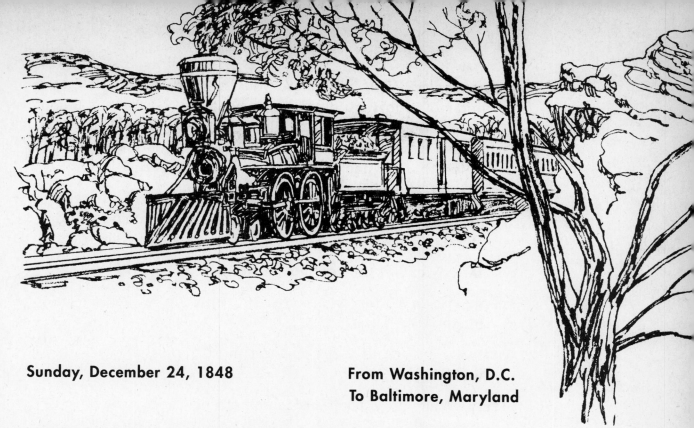

Sunday, December 24, 1848

**From Washington, D.C.
To Baltimore, Maryland**

NARRATOR: In Washington, William and Ellen hurried off to catch the train for Baltimore. They arrived in Baltimore on the evening of December 24. They had reached the most perilous stop on their long journey.

ELLEN: Baltimore frightens me more than I can say, William. I should be happy that it's the last southern port we have to travel through. But I am more anxious than ever.

WILLIAM: We got good reason for being fearful. The guards are everywhere on the lookout to keep slaves from crossing into Pennsylvania where they'd be free. But I can't believe we'll fail—not when we're so near our goal!

NARRATOR: William helped his master into the train. Then he made his way to the Negro car in the back. Suddenly, he felt someone tapping his shoulder.

CONDUCTOR 2: Where are you going?

WILLIAM: To Philadelphia, sir.

CONDUCTOR 2: What are you going there for?

WILLIAM: I'm traveling with my master, sir. He's in a carriage up front, sir.

CONDUCTOR 2: Well, I calculate you had better get him out, and be mighty quick about it because the train will soon be starting. It's against railroad rules to let any man take a slave past here, unless he can satisfy them in the office that he has a right to take him along.

NARRATOR: William ran back to the carriage where he had left Ellen. Fortunately, "Mr. Johnson" was sitting quite alone.

WILLIAM: How're you feeling, master?

ELLEN: Much better, thank you. I'm glad we're getting on so nicely.

WILLIAM: I'm afraid we're not getting on quite so well as we'd hoped.

ELLEN: What do you mean? Is something the matter?

WILLIAM: Mr. Johnson, sir, we gotta go into the station and prove I'm your slave.

ELLEN: [*whispering*] Prove that you're my slave? But I have no proof! Oh, William, we've come so far! Is it possible that we're doomed after all to hopeless bondage?

WILLIAM: [*whispering*] Ellen, now's the time we gotta call up our faith and courage. We'd best go in . . . and quickly.

NARRATOR: The two terror-stricken fugitives entered the station office. They both knew that their very existence was at stake; with this encounter, they would sink or swim. The office was crowded with travelers full of Christmas cheer. William and Ellen made their way to the station master's window. He eyed them suspiciously, but somehow Ellen managed to kept her head up and her voice firm.

ELLEN: Do you wish to see me, sir?

STATION MASTER: Yes. I hear you're traveling with a slave. It's against railroad rules, sir, to allow any person to take a slave out of Baltimore into Philadelphia, unless he can satisfy us that he has a right to take him along.

ELLEN: Why is that?

Macmillan/McGraw-Hill

STATION MASTER: Because, sir, if we should allow any gentleman to take a slave past here into Philadelphia, and should that gentleman not be the slave's owner, and should the proper master come and prove that his slave escaped on our railroad—then we would have to pay what the slave was worth. That's why!

ELLEN: I understand, sir, but . . .

STATION MASTER: Now, do you, or do you not, have proof that this is your slave?

ELLEN: I do, sir, but I do not have it with me.

NARRATOR: Their conversation had attracted the attention of the other passengers, who seemed to sympathize with "Mr. Johnson" because he looked so ill. Seeing their reaction, the station master became more polite.

STATION MASTER: Do you have some acquaintance in Baltimore who could assure us that this slave is your property?

ELLEN: Alas no, sir, I do not. I bought tickets in Charleston to pass us through to Philadelphia, and therefore you have no right to detain us here in Baltimore.

STATION MASTER: Well, sir, right or not, I shan't let you go through without proof that this is your slave!

NARRATOR: For a few minutes, there was total silence in the office. Ellen and William looked at each other. Neither dared speak a word for fear of making some blunder that would give them away. They knew that the railroad officers had the power to throw them into prison. Then they would be taken back to punishment and a life of slavery. They felt as though they were suspended over a pit by the thinnest of threads. Then suddenly, a large man pushed to the front of the crowd and approached the station master's window.

ONLOOKER: Where's your Christmas spirit, station master? Can't you see that this poor gentleman is sick. Have a heart. Let him go on to Philadelphia.

STATION MASTER: That's easy for you to say, sir. It's not you who's taking the responsibility.

NARRATOR: Just then the bell rang for the train to leave. It came with the sudden shock of an earthquake. The office door opened; the conductor of the train stepped in. Every eye was fixed intently on the drama at the station master's window.

STATION MASTER: Conductor, did these two come with you on the train from Washington?

CONDUCTOR 2: They surely did, sir! Going up to Philadelphia to see a special doctor, I understand. All right, everyone, we're ready to pull out.

NARRATOR: "Mr. Johnson" appealed to the station master once again.

ELLEN: Please allow me to board that train, sir. I am feeling faint and very weak.

STATION MASTER: I really don't know what to do. . . . Oh-h-h, I calculate it's all right. Clerk, inform the conductor to let this gentleman and his slave pass. As he is not well, it's a pity to stop him here. We will let him go.

ELLEN: Thank you, sir. Thank you! And a very Merry Christmas to you and your family.

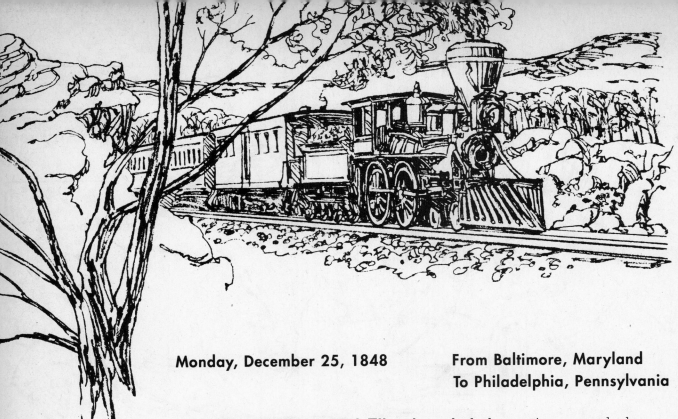

Monday, December 25, 1848   **From Baltimore, Maryland To Philadelphia, Pennsylvania**

NARRATOR: William and Ellen boarded the train seconds before it pulled out of the station. Ellen collapsed into her seat. The train traveled on into the night, carrying them closer and closer to their final destination. Early on Christmas morning, the train pulled into the Philadelphia station. Before it even stopped, William leaped onto the platform and ran to get Ellen.

ELLEN: We are safe, William! Safe and free!

WILLIAM: Glory be, Ellen! We have been granted freedom for Christmas!

NARRATOR: The abolitionist William Lloyd Garrison recounted the Craft's harrowing escape in his newspaper, *The Liberator*. In 1850, two years after their flight to freedom, Ellen and William Craft moved to England for fear that if they stayed in the United States, they might be forced to return to their former masters under the provisions of the soon-to-be-enacted Fugitive Slave Act. With the assistance of a friend, William wrote a book titled *Running a Thousand Miles for Freedom*, which recounted the true story of their daring escape. The Crafts and their two children lived in England for eighteen years. They returned to the United States after the Civil War and bought a former plantation near Savannah, Georgia. There they established a school for black children and adults.

Blocking Diagram

Arrange sixteen chairs, as shown. The narrator can use a music stand to hold the script.

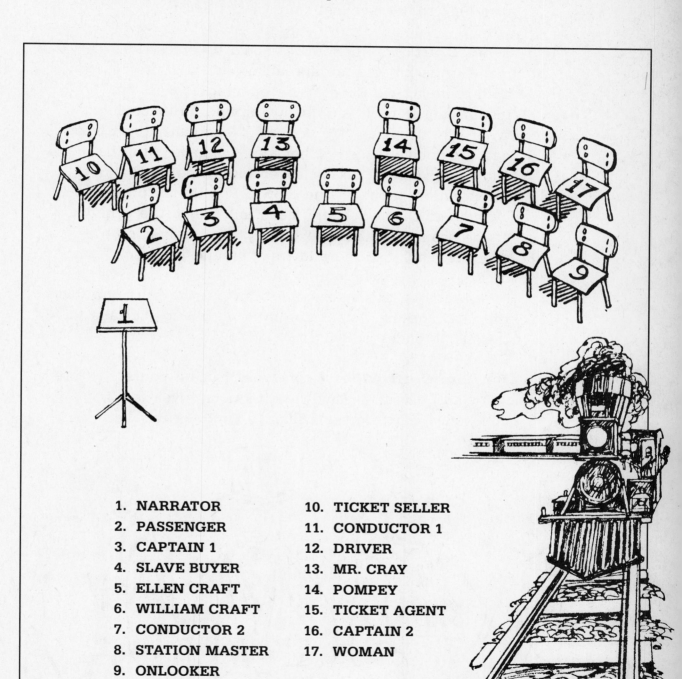

1. NARRATOR
2. PASSENGER
3. CAPTAIN 1
4. SLAVE BUYER
5. ELLEN CRAFT
6. WILLIAM CRAFT
7. CONDUCTOR 2
8. STATION MASTER
9. ONLOOKER

10. TICKET SELLER
11. CONDUCTOR 1
12. DRIVER
13. MR. CRAY
14. POMPEY
15. TICKET AGENT
16. CAPTAIN 2
17. WOMAN

Costume Suggestions

Narrator Although this role does not call for a special costume, a string tie for a boy or a long skirt for a girl may help the reader feel more in character.

Ellen Craft This performer should be dressed as a man—in dark pants, a dark jacket, and a white blouse with a cravat. As Ellen in the opening scenes, the reader can drape a large shawl around her shoulders. When she becomes "Mr. Johnson," she can put on a top hat, previously placed at her feet. To make a top hat, cut a long strip of six- or seven-inch-wide black construction paper for the crown. Roll the strip into a cylinder to fit the reader's head and staple the cylinder at the seam. To make the brim, place the crown on a sheet of black oak tag and trace around its base. Then draw a larger circle around the first one. Draw six or seven tabs on the inner circle. Cut out the brim and fold the tabs upright. Attach the brim by gluing the tabs to the inside of the crown.

William Craft William can dress in dark pants, a white shirt, and a vest. Follow the directions given for "Mr. Johnson's" hat to make William's white beaver hat.

Macmillan/McGraw-Hill

Mr. Cray, Passenger, Slave Buyer, and Onlooker
The basic costumes for these readers can consist of long
pants, shirts, and jackets. An additional item such as a
cravat, string tie, vest, or hat will help individualize
each outfit.

Railroad Employees These performers can wear dark
pants, white shirts, and dark jackets. A cap with the
employee's job designation would help differentiate the
various characters.

Captain 1 and Captain 2 Light pants, dark jackets,
and blue caps with nautical insignias on the front would
be appropriate for the captains.

Driver and Pompey These readers can wear jeans,
work shirts, and suspenders.

Woman A long dress, or a frilly blouse and a long skirt,
would be fine for this character. An umbrella decorated
to resemble a parasol can be placed near her chair.

A Perilous Journey

Ellen and William Craft's thousand-mile flight to freedom took place more than one hundred and forty years ago. Their route and means of transportation are illustrated on this map.

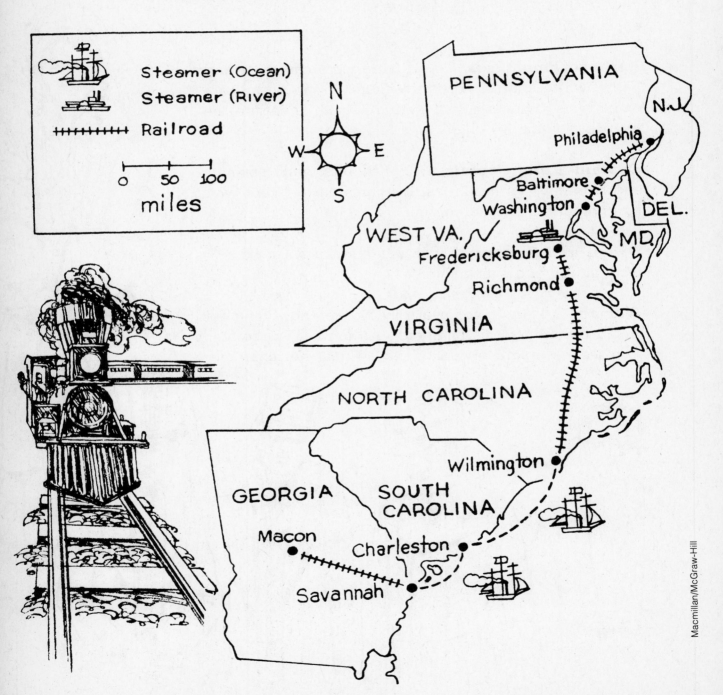

Readers Theater Play

After your students have participated in a Readers Theater production or two, many may be motivated to write a Readers Theater script of their own. The following five student resource pages are designed to help guide them through this process.

In addition to developing writing skills, creating a Readers Theater script is also a useful way to extend students' study of story elements. In creating any Readers Theater script, students must solve the problem of conveying action and changes in time and place in a script that is read rather than acted with costumes, scenes, and props. The transformation of narrative into drama also challenges students to closely examine elements of character, motivation, plot, and setting. If students are adapting a story, they must determine what to include and what to omit. If they are writing an original play, they face a different set of decisions: how to invent a story line that incorporates dramatic tension and how to make characters believable. If the play is based on historical events, students should determine what research is required to ensure historical accuracy.

Before students begin writing their own Readers Theater plays, you may find it helpful to explore with them the differences between narrative and drama. One way to do this is to obtain a copy of *The Secret Garden,* by Frances Hodgson Burnett or *Tom Sawyer,* by Mark Twain (sources are listed in the Bibliography on page xii).

Read portions from one of these selections and invite comparisons with the Readers Theater version found in this book. You may wish to assist students in evaluating the relative merits of telling the story in each form. What is gained in each case? What is lost? In making these comparisons, focus on the role of the narrator in providing transitions from one setting to another and in describing action that cannot be conveyed through dialog in the Readers Theater version. Point out examples of how descriptions and other elements of the narrative are transformed into dialog, and how some characters in the play may seem more real because of the words they speak.

After students grasp the major differences between stories and scripts, introduce the following Readers Theater writing-process worksheets to guide them through the process of creating their own Readers Theater plays. Students can work individually, in small cooperative-writing groups, or as an entire class when writing a script.

If your students choose to adapt a folk tale or legend, suggest that they read several versions of the story before they begin the writing process. If students decide to adapt a story or a book, a reading followed by group discussion will ensure that all students are familiar with the story plot, characters, and setting. If students choose to write an original play, they will need to create the plot, characters, and setting themselves.

Getting Started

Stop a minute to think about the Readers Theater productions in which you've participated. As a member of a Readers Theater group, you may have thought that you too could write a play for others to read. Writing a play is not that complicated if you follow a series of steps that take you from finding an idea for a play through writing the final script.

FINAL SCRIPT
DIALOG
CHARACTERS
SETTING
PLOT
PLAY IDEA

Getting an idea for a play

At one time or another, every writer has asked the question, "What should I write about?" One of the most important steps in writing a play is coming up with an idea that will work. A play is like any other story—it generally grows from real-life *experiences* combined with input from your imagination. If you take a little time to think about your experiences, you'll find dozens of things that could be used in a play. Here are a few real-life experiences that can provide good sources for ideas:

- personal experiences you've had at home, at school, or just about anywhere
- experiences that have happened to friends, family members, or others you know
- things you've read in books, newspapers, and magazines
- things you've seen in television programs and movies
- things you've read about in history books

Macmillan/McGraw-Hill

Besides real-life experiences, the other ingredient that goes into creating an idea for a play is your *imagination*. Your imagination is different from that of anyone else—it's one of the things that makes you unique! No one else will imagine exactly the same things in the same way. Your imagination enables you to start with a real-life experience and then transform it into something that no one else could think of.

A Friend's Experience: Last year, my friend's class put on a school play. He told me that the star was so concerned about his role that, in his view, everyone else's part was unimportant.

Imagination: Suppose someone was so serious about a role in a play that his or her behavior became annoying to everyone in the family. What kinds of problems might arise? How would the family deal with these problems?

Get together with a partner or a small group. Brainstorm at least one idea for each source listed above. In each case, add a comment about how your imagination might allow you to treat the idea in an original way. Use the back of this page or another sheet of paper to record your ideas. To help you get started, one possibility has been done for you.

THE PLOT

A play is made up of related events that tell a story. This series of events is called the plot. A good plot will keep you asking, "What's going to happen next?"

Most plots consist of three parts:

- A situation, in which the characters and the setting are introduced
- A conflict, which involves the characters in an attempt to solve some problem. The problem might involve only the characters or may be a struggle against some outside force, such as nature.
- A resolution, or solution, to the conflict

Macmillan/McGraw-Hill

When you're trying to think of plot ideas, remember that all three parts of the plot do not need to be the same length. In most plays, the basic situation is introduced in a page or two. Similarly, the resolution is often presented very concisely. Usually, the majority of events spelled out in the plot focus on the conflict.

Here's a possible plot outline for the incident involving a girl preparing for a starring role in a play, which was mentioned on the "Getting Started" page.

Situation: Jenny has just learned that she will play Dorothy in a school production of The Wizard of Oz. She is thrilled with the role and is determined to do an outstanding job. The same week, her younger brother, Alan, announces that he will be playing a tree in a kindergarten production scheduled for Earth Day.

Conflict: Although Jenny's parents are pleased with her announcement, they treat her role about the same as they treat Alan's. This baffles and upsets Jenny, who feels her part is much more significant. A number of incidents occur involving preparations for both productions in which the children express their annoyance with each other.

Resolution: Finally their mother, who has tried to mediate the disagreements between Jenny and Alan, takes out a photo album and shows pictures of a kindergarten play from some years earlier in which Jenny played one of seven rabbits. The photos and subsequent discussion help Jenny recall how she felt when she was Alan's age. Jenny realizes that any role, regardless of size, is important.

Look again at the list you made when you read the "Getting Started" page. From the list, choose your favorite play idea. Then write a plot outline based on the idea you've chosen. Your outline should include a summary of the situation, the conflict, and the resolution. Write your plot outline on the back of this page or on another sheet of paper.

CREATING CHARACTERS

Anyone who appears in a play is called a character. Usually characters are people; however, in fantasies or fables, animals and elements of nature such as flowers or a river can have speaking parts. When writing a play, it is important to try to make your characters different from one another. These differences can help you create a conflict and keep the play action moving forward.

Think about the stories and books you've read. In these works, writers can tell readers about the characters. In some instances, the writer may stop the action to describe what a character is like or why a character is behaving in a certain way.

Macmillan/McGraw-Hill

A play is different. The only way information can be shared about characters is through dialog, the words spoken by the characters. Through dialog, the audience learns what the different characters are like. What does this mean to you, as the writer? It means you must have a clear idea of each character in your mind as you write your play. It also means you will want to carefully choose the words said by your characters to make sure they fit your view of each character's personality. One way to get a clear idea of each personality is to write *character sketches*. A character sketch is a description of a character's appearance, personality, and relationship to the other people in the story. Here, for example, is a character sketch of Jenny's brother Alan.

Alan is a five year old boy who can be adorable one moment and infuriating the next. He looks like most boys his age, except he has bright red hair and a grin that makes him look like a jack o'lantern because of his three missing teeth! Usually, Alan is a great little brother -- he's funny, friendly, and smart. But sometimes he can be a real pain, especially when he feels that not enough attention is being paid to him. Then he whines, fusses, and tattles on his older sister Jenny. Life with Alan can be difficult at times, because no one can predict what he will be like from one minute to the next.

Look back at the plot you have outlined for your play. Then make a list of the main characters you'll need to create. Write a short character sketch for each. Remember that the more information you include, the easier it will be to invent dialog for your character. Keep these sketches handy as you work on your play to remind you of what each person is like. This will help you write believable dialog for your play.

A READERS THEATER SCRIPT

Writing a play is different from writing a story. One important difference you've already discovered is the exclusive use of dialog in a play. Another important difference is in the format. In a script, the characters' names appear on the left followed by a colon (:). The dialog appears on the right side of the page. A third important difference is the use of a narrator in many Readers Theater plays. A narrator can be used to describe a scene, identify changes in setting, or describe important actions that cannot be written as dialog.

Study the following example based on the play idea described in preceding pages. Pay special attention to the part of the narrator.

Narrator: Alan was in the living room with his parents, busily working on his tree costume for the kindergarten play. At that moment, Jenny came in the front door, reading from her script.

Jenny: "Goodness, Toto! This doesn't look anything like Kansas!" Oh, hello, everyone. I was just rehearsing one of my big scenes.

Alan: We were just making my costume. It's for my big scene.

Macmillan/McGraw-Hill

Jenny: You mean as a tree? He doesn't seem to understand, does he mother?

Mother: Understand what, dear?

Jenny: What it means to have a real part in a play.

Alan: I do have a real part! I'm a tree, and that's more real than a girl whose best friend is a talking scarecrow!

Jenny: Oh, right! And what will you do, make tree noises? A real character is when you have lines like, "There's no place like home!"

Father: That's a good line, all right. But Alan has lines of his own to memorize.

Alan: I'll say I do. Just listen to this! "I help make the oxygen you need to breathe."

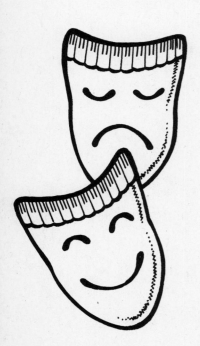

Use the dialog above to discuss these questions in your Readers Theater group.

- How might a story about this incident be told? How is the script different from a story version?
- What is the purpose of the narrator's speech?
- Is the dialog appropriate for the characters?
- What do you think the characters will say next?

Create a scene for your play in which several important characters interact. Use your character sketches as a guide in writing dialog for the characters you've chosen. Use the narrator to describe actions that are not part of the dialog or to establish the setting.

READY, SET, WRITE

Use the following checklist as a guide in planning and writing your play. After you complete each step, put a check in the box.

PREWRITING

☐ Brainstorm ideas for a play.
☐ Outline the plot.
☐ Decide on the setting.
☐ Write the character sketches.

DRAFTING

☐ Write a first draft of your play. If you work in a group, one person can record the dialog as the group dictates it.
☐ Set up your script using play format. Place the characters' names on the left and the dialog on the right.
☐ Use the narrator to describe any action that cannot be written as dialog and to tell about changes in time or setting.
☐ Think of a title for your play.

REVISING

☐ Make sure the events in your play follow one another in logical order.
☐ Check to see that you have included all the information the audience will need to make sense of the play.
☐ Add or eliminate characters, as needed.
☐ Read your play aloud. Rewrite any dialog that does not sound natural.
☐ Add expressions that help bring your characters to life.
☐ Add humorous dialog, if appropriate.

Macmillan/McGraw-Hill

PROOFREADING

☐ Correct all mistakes in spelling, grammar, punctuation, and script form.

☐ Ask someone else to proofread your script for errors you may have missed.

PUBLISHING

☐ Make a final draft of the script. It should be neat and easy to read. If possible, prepare it on a typewriter or a word processor. Check to make sure that you have made all corrections.

☐ Make a copy for each member of the cast.

When your script is finished, it's time to begin rehearsing. At this point, try not to think of your play as finished. During rehearsals, you may find some places where changes could improve the play. When you're satisfied, plan a performance to share your work with an audience. Don't forget to step forward and take a curtain call for all your hard work as author!

CHORAL READING ▶▶▶▶

LEVEL 12/UNIT 1

Spelling Bee

group 1   group 2

solo   1   2   3

LEVEL 12/UNIT 3

IT COULDN'T BE DONE

group 1   group 2   group 3

solo   1   2   3   4   5   6

LEVEL 12/UNIT 2

THUMBPRINT

group 1   group 2

solo   1   2   3   4   5   6   7

LEVEL 12/UNIT 2

BOOKS FALL OPEN

boys   girls

BLOCKING DIAGRAMS

LEVEL 12/UNIT 4

No
Present
Like
The
Time

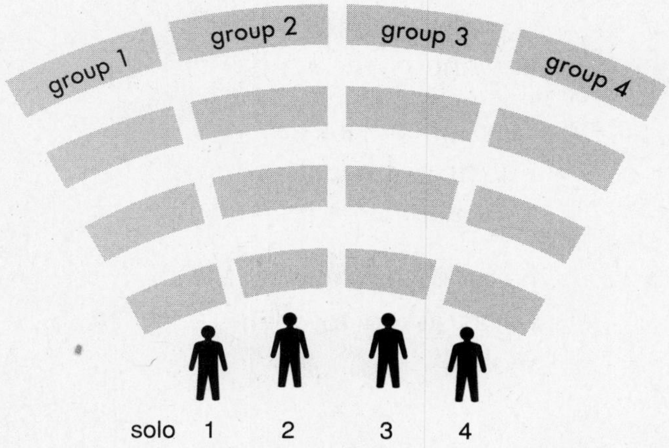

group 1

group 2

group 3

group 4

solo   1   2   3   4

LEVEL 12/UNIT 5

Something for Everyone

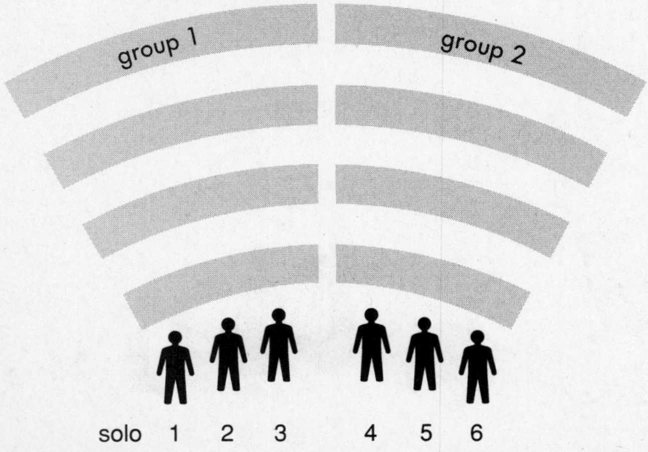

group 1

group 2

solo   1   2   3   4   5   6

LEVEL 12/UNIT 6

Give Me Liberty, or Give Me Death

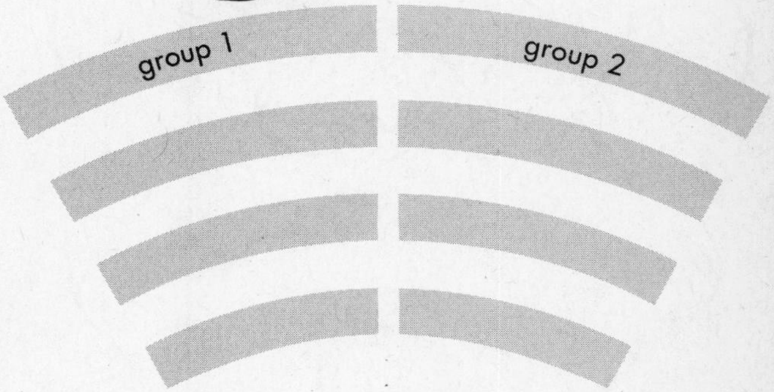

group 1

group 2

LEVEL 12/UNIT 6

from

The Declaration of Independence

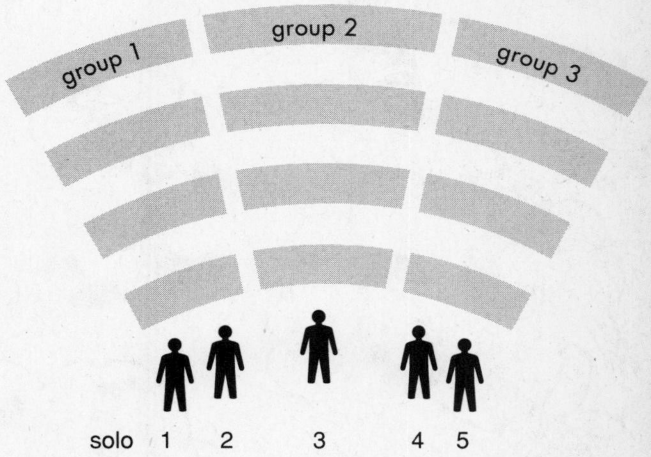

group 1

group 2

group 3

solo   1   2   3   4   5

Spelling Bee

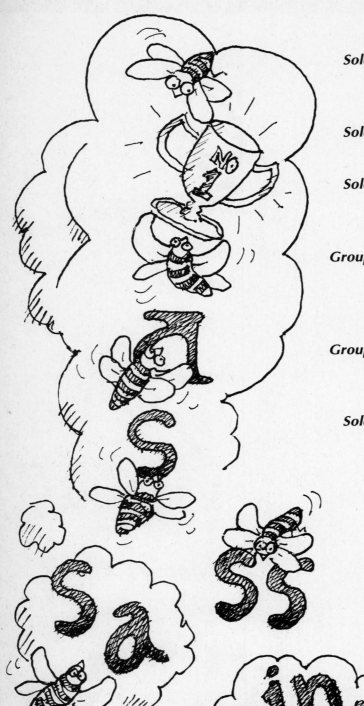

Solo 1: Best speller since third grade
that Beaver Elementary
had ever seen

Solo 2: Could spell *assassination*
when I was nine.

Solo 3: When I was eleven
entered the
Big Spelling Bee.

Group 1: Winning would mean
a try at the
county championship
and then—the world.

Group 2: Everyone knew I'd win.
But first, I had to
win at Beaver.

Solo 1: Nervous beyond words,
I was asked to spell
woke.

Solo 2: Sputtered W-O-A-K.

Solo 3: WOAK.

Group 1: Knew I'd blown it,
just nervous,
but made them check a
dictionary, anyway,
to save myself some
dignity

Group 2: and on the chance that
some stupid idiot
like me
had used it in a
spelling bee
and made it
a word.

All: It wasn't.

Cynthia Rylant

THUMBPRINT

All: In the heel of my thumb
are whorls, whirls, wheels
in a unique design:
mine alone.
What a treasure to own!

Group 1: My own flesh, my own feelings.
No other, however grand or base,
can ever contain the same.

Solo 1: My signature,
Solo 2: thumbing the pages of my time.
Solo 3: My universe key,
Solo 4: my singularity.
Solo 5: Impress, implant,
Solo 6: I am myself,
Solo 7: of all my atom parts I am the sum.

Group 2: And out of my blood and my brain
I make my own interior weather,
my own sun and rain.

All: Imprint my mark upon the world,
whatever I shall become.

Eve Merriam

BOOKS FALL OPEN

All: Books fall open,
you fall in,
delighted where
you've never been;

Girls: hear voices not once
heard before,
reach world on world
through door on door;

Boys: find unexpected
keys to things
locked up beyond
imaginings.

Girls: What *might* you be,
perhaps *become*,
because one book
is somewhere?

Boys: Some
wise delver into
wisdom, wit,
and wherewithal
has written it.

David McCord

IT COULDN'T BE DONE

Group 1: Somebody said that it couldn't be done,
But he with a chuckle replied
That "maybe it couldn't," but he would be one
Who wouldn't say so till he'd tried.
So he buckled right in with the trace of a grin
On his face. If he worried he hid it.

All: He started to sing as he tackled the thing
That couldn't be done, and he did it.

Group 2: Somebody scoffed: "Oh, you'll never do that;
At least no one ever has done it";
But he took off his coat and he took off his hat,
And the first thing we knew he'd begun it.
With a lift of his chin and a bit of a grin,
Without any doubting or quiddit,

All: He started to sing as he tackled the thing
That couldn't be done, and he did it.

Group 3: There are thousands to tell you it cannot be done,
There are thousands to prophesy failure;
There are thousands to point out to you, one by one,
The dangers that wait to assail you.
But just buckle in with a bit of a grin,
Just take off your coat and go to it;

All: Just start to sing as you tackle the thing
That "cannot be done," and you'll do it.

Edgar A. Guest

GET A TRANSFER

Solo 1: If you are on the Gloomy Line,
    All: Get a transfer.
Solo 2: If you're inclined to fret and pine,
    All: Get a transfer.
Group 1: Get off the track of doubt and gloom,
        Get on the sunshine Track—there's room—
    All: Get a transfer.

Solo 3: If you're on the Worry Train,
    All: Get a transfer.
Solo 4: You must not stay there and complain,
    All: Get a transfer.
Group 2: The Cheerful Cars are passing through,
        And there's lots of room for you—
    All: Get a transfer.

Solo 5: If you're on the Grouchy Track,
    All: Get a transfer.
Solo 6: Just take a Happy Special back,
    All: Get a transfer.
Group 3: Jump on the train and pull the rope,
        That lands you at the station Hope—
    All: Get a transfer.

Unknown

NO PRESENT LIKE THE TIME

All: "No time like the present," they always used to say,
Meaning—

Solo 1: *Get Busy!*

Solo 2: *Do You Hear Me?*

Solo 3: *Don't Delay!*

All: Much better in reverse (it doesn't have to rhyme):
Simply, simply,

Solo 4: *No present like the time.*

Group 1: Time, you agree, is everybody's gift,
But the packages aren't the same.
The lid of each is there to lift,
Yet only one package bears your name.

Group 2: Lift the lid a little now each morning,
And what comes whistling out?
A day's supply of time. Almost a-borning
It dies with every breath as you go about
Your work or play.

Group 3: How much of it is in
That package? No one knows. You, least of all.
Time is indifferent to what we begin;
Indifferent also to whether we stand or fall.

All: Don't waste your time, they say. Waste time you will;
And such as you wish, of course, is yours to squander.

Group 4: Don't call it wasted when you climb a hill.
Through fields and woods to wander
Is to be young, and time belongs to the young.
It's when you're old that clocks begin to tick.

All: Play fair with time: his praise so rarely sung.
He is your snail. But oh, his pulse is quick.

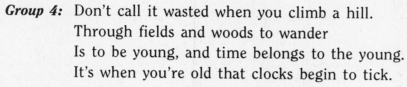

David McCord

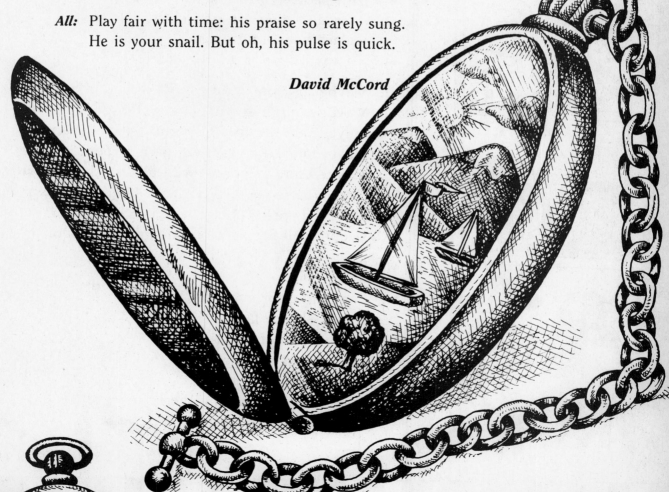

Something for Everyone

All: Something for everyone,
that's when a family's fun.
Group 1: There's lots of surprises,
with different sizes
and shapes to a family.
All: Something for sharing there,
with people caring there.
Group 2: It's a door you can go in,
a place you can grow in.
It's anything you need it to be.

Solo 1: Maybe it's your mother and your dad and you.
Solo 2: Maybe you have one place or divide it in two.
Solo 3: Maybe there's a brother or a sis who shares.
Solo 4: Maybe there's a grandma with a room upstairs.
Solo 5: Maybe there's an aunt with all her children grown.
Solo 6: Maybe there's a stepdad with kids of his own.
Group 1: Maybe there's a cousin, even three or four,
sleeping all together on one great big floor.

All: But there's

All: Something for everyone,
that's when a family's fun.
Group 1: There's lots of surprises,
with different sizes
and shapes to a family.
All: Something for sharing there,
with people caring there.

Group 2: It's a door you can go in,
a place you can grow in.
It's anything you need it to be.

Solo 1: Living in a castle or a riverboat,
Solo 2: living in a farmhouse with a billy goat,
Solo 3: living in an igloo or an Indian tent,
Solo 4: living in a small apartment—paying rent,
Solo 5: living on a mountain where the sky is blue,
Solo 6: living in a one-room with a window view. . . .
Group 2: No, it's not the people or the place
they live.
It's more the kind of feeling and the
love they give.
All: But there's

All: Something for everyone,
that's when a family's fun.
Group 1: There's lots of surprises,
with different sizes
and shapes to a family.
All: Something for sharing there,
with people caring there.
Group 2: It's a door you can go in,
a place you can grow in.
It's anything you need it to be.

All: Something for everyone!

Carol Hall

Give Me Liberty, or Give Me Death

All: Gentlemen may cry, Peace Peace
but there is no pease.

Group 1: The war is actually begun!
The next gale that sweeps from the north will bring
to our ears the clash of resounding arms!

Group 2: Our brethren are already in the field!
Why stand we here idle?

Group 1: What is it that gentlemen wish?
What would they have?

Group 2: Is life so dear, or peace so sweet,
as to be purchased at the price of chains and slavery?

All: Forbid it, Almighty God!
I know not what course others may take;
but as for me,

Group 1: give me liberty,

Group 2: or give me death!

Patrick Henry

—From *The Call to Arms*, a speech delivered March 23, 1775, to the Virginia House of Burgesses, Richmond, Virginia

Macmillan/McGraw-Hill

from

The Declaration of Independence

July 4, 1776

Group 1: When, in the course of human events, it becomes necessary for one people to dissolve the political bands which have connected them with another,

Group 2: and to assume among the powers of the earth, the separate and equal station to which the laws of nature and of nature's God entitle them,

Group 3: a decent respect to the opinions of mankind requires that they should declare the causes which impel them to the separation.

All: We hold these truths to be self-evident:

Solo 1: That all men are created equal,

Solo 2: that they are endowed by their Creator with certian unalienable rights,

Solo 3: that among these are life, liberty, and the pursuit of happiness;

Solo 4: that, to secure these rights, Governments are instituted among men, deriving their just powers from the consent of the governed;

Solo 5: that, whenever any form of Government becomes destructive of these ends, it is the right of the people to alter or to abolish it, and to institute new Government,

All: laying its foundation on such principles, and organizing its powers in such form, as to them shall seem most likely to effect their safety and happiness.

When you perform in a Readers Theater production, you may think of yourself primarily as a reader. Yet in Readers Theater, you are also a listener and a team member. Your performance in all three areas contributes to the success of the production.

Use this sheet to help you evaluate your performance in each area.

Oral-Reading Skills

	ALWAYS	MOST OF THE TIME	SOMETIMES	ALMOST NEVER	NEVER
Did I read my lines fluently?	1	2	3	4	5
Did I check for pronunciation of unfamiliar words?	1	2	3	4	5
Did I mark my script for pauses and for special emphasis?	1	2	3	4	5
Did I observe punctuation marks and pause marks in my script?	1	2	3	4	5
Did I read with expression?	1	2	3	4	5
Did I vary my reading rate depending on the meaning?	1	2	3	4	5
Did I vary my pitch, according to the mood of the play?	1	2	3	4	5
Did I work on my diction, pronouncing beginnings and endings of words carefully and clearly?	1	2	3	4	5
Did I project my voice so I could be heard?	1	2	3	4	5
Did I familiarize myself with my script so I could use on-stage and off-stage focus?	1	2	3	4	5

Listening Skills

	ALWAYS	MOST OF THE TIME	SOMETIMES	ALMOST NEVER	NEVER
Did I listen attentively for my cues and come in on time?	1	2	3	4	5
Did I listen to myself as I read, making adjustments in rate, pitch, or diction as necessary?	1	2	3	4	5
Did I listen attentively as others read, avoiding any distracting sounds and movements?	1	2	3	4	5
Did I listen to the audience and allow time for their reactions?	1	2	3	4	5
Did I visualize the action and the setting of the play?	1	2	3	4	5

Teamwork Skills

	ALWAYS	MOST OF THE TIME	SOMETIMES	ALMOST NEVER	NEVER
Did I come to my Readers Theater team prepared to contribute?	1	2	3	4	5
Did I allow others to express themselves in discussions?	1	2	3	4	5
Did I show respect for the opinions of others?	1	2	3	4	5
Did I make my suggestions to others constructive?	1	2	3	4	5
Did I consider the suggestions of my teammates?	1	2	3	4	5

List two or three suggestions you received from teammates.

Explain how one of these suggestions helped you improve your performance.

Select a personal goal for your next production and write about it.

Select a team goal for your next production and write about it.

Macmillan/McGraw-Hill